THE WAY OF THE ATHLETE

THE WAY OF THE ATHLETE

The Role of Sports in Building Character for Academic, Business, and Personal Success

Rob Pate

SKYHORSE PUBLISHING

Skyhorse Publishing books may be purchased in bulk at special discounts for sales promotion, corporate gifts, fund-raising, or educational purposes. Special editions can also be created to specifications. For details, contact the Special Sales Department, Skyhorse Publishing, 307 West 36th Street, 11th Floor, New York, NY 10018 or info@skyhorse-publishing.com.

Skyhorse® and Skyhorse Publishing® are registered trademarks of Skyhorse Publishing, Inc.®, a Delaware corporation.

Visit our website at www.skyhorsepublishing.com.

10 9 8 7 6 5 4 3 2 1

Library of Congress Cataloging-in-Publication Data is available on file.

Cover design: Richard Rossiter

All interior photos courtesy of the Auburn University Athletic Department.

ISBN: 978-1-62914-804-5

Ebook ISBN: 978-1-63220-183-6

Printed in the United States of America

Dedication

I dedicate this book to the many influential coaches who have built countless athletes into better people.

Special Thanks

To the many former teammates, coaches, friends, and fellow Auburn players of different eras, I am indebted to you for your significant contributions. Your stories and insight personalize each characteristic I discuss, and each of you has positively impacted my path along the way.

To Phillip Marshall, the undisputed and acclaimed voice of Auburn insight, I thank you for your prologue. Having covered countless Auburn athletes for decades, your view and commentary are immeasurably valued.

To my wife, Dana, for listening to my writing at all the various stages and encouraging me to finish what I started. Her prayers and support are unceasing.

To Kirk Sampson, associate athletic director/communications, and Scott Scoggins of Auburn Athletics for their willingness to help in this endeavor. Kirk is a longtime friend and the best in the business; he directed me to Scott for the photographs I needed. Scott sent me every single photo used in this book within fifteen minutes of me asking.

To the many coaches who chiseled away at my being, enhancing me in ways I never dreamed.

To my children, for your inspiration—I love you!

To my parents, for their example.

Thank you.

TABLE OF CONTENTS

FOREWORD

by Phillip Marshall

It was an introduction unlike any Joe Whitt, Auburn's outside linebackers coach, had experienced. In early 1983, a young man he'd never met walked into his office.

"Hey, Coach, I'm Kevin Greene and I'm your starting outside linebacker," the young man said.

Pat Dye was heading into his third season as Auburn's head coach. The Tigers would win the SEC championship later that year. Just making the team would be a challenge.

"He looked the part, but I thought, 'This guy is out of his mind,'" Whitt said. "More times than not, a guy will fall on his face. He didn't. You could tell the first day of spring practice that he was different. He didn't know anything about what he was doing, but he was tough and he was a banger. From there, the rest is history."

In 1983, Greene played outside linebacker behind Quency Williams and Gerald Robinson. Midway through his senior season in 1984, he became a starter. He led the team in sacks with 10½, and won the Zeke Smith Award as Auburn's Defensive

Player of the Year. The Los Angeles Rams chose him with the first pick of the fifth round in the 1985 NFL Draft.

Greene played for the Rams, the Pittsburgh Steelers, the San Francisco 49ers, and the Carolina Panthers. His flowing blond mane and ferocious intensity made him a star and a crowd favorite everywhere he played. He had double-digit sacks in ten of his fifteen seasons.

That wouldn't have seemed possible when Greene walked on to Auburn's football team for the first time in 1980, and walked away a few weeks later.

Greene was a scout team halfback. He'd been late reporting because he'd joined the National Guard, spending three months in basic training and attending military police academy. He'd started off behind, and had decided the time wasn't right. He told his coaches he was going to concentrate on his education.

Some three years later, a conversation between Greene and assistant strength coach Paul White changed everything. White, who worked out at Kaz Gym in Auburn, told Whitt he'd seen a young man who wanted to play football and looked like he could. Whitt asked White to tell the young man to stop by and see him.

By that time, Greene had tested himself more than many of those who played. He'd moved from the National Guard to the Army Reserve, and was already a second lieutenant. Since he'd last been on the field, Greene had grown from 202 pounds to 232. He'd gotten stronger, and had lost none of his speed and quickness.

"You know what? I wanted it," Greene said. "I wanted it more than other people. I've always said I would go to war with a walk-on more than a scholarship player. A walk-on has to scrap for everything. I've seen more drive, desire, passion and determination in walk-ons' eyes than anybody else's.

The philosophy I live by is that, if you have fire in your heart, it will compensate for any lack of ability. Coach Whitt worked really hard with me. I think he saw that fire in my eyes and passion in my heart."

Greene didn't walk on at Auburn with thoughts of playing in the NFL. He just wanted to play. It was Auburn football, he said, that convinced him he could do it and taught him how to do it.

"What prepared me for the NFL was the work ethic and hard-nosed, ass-kicking football I learned under Pat Dye," Greene said. "What we went through in the spring was so violent and intense and physical. It was evident a couple of days into my first NFL training camp that I was rocking people's worlds, because Pat Dye had us moving at another level and hitting at another level."

Growing up in a military family, Greene seldom lived in one place for a long time, but there were two constants in his life: love of country, and love of Auburn University. His parents had grown up near Aniston. His father had joined the army out of Jacksonville State University, but the Greenes were always an Auburn family. "We had Auburn in our hearts," Greene said.

On January 27, 2000, some seventeen years after he walked boldly into Whitt's office, Greene announced his retirement.

"I always wanted to go out on my own terms," Greene recalled. "I think I'm doing that. I'm going out on top."

Greene never lost the walk-on mentality, the belief that he would work harder and longer than anyone else.

"It's all heart, drive, desire, determination, and commitment," Greene emphasized. "That's the creed I live by. I was the first to come to the stadium and the last to leave. I knew my opponent. I knew what personnel groupings were. I was a student of the game. Not only that; I took it very, very seriously."

Greene returned to football to coach for the Green Bay Packers, but left in 2014 to spend more time with his wife and children. He's been a semi-finalist in balloting for the Pro Football Hall of Fame nine times. He is a member of the Alabama Sports Hall of Fame.

"Sometimes people forget where they came from," Whitt said. "Kevin never did and never has. He was very intelligent. You couldn't give him too much to do, couldn't ask him to do it too many times. He was always excited about getting better."

Greene's story is one of thousands that form the fabric of Auburn football. For more than a century, from small towns and large, from farms and from housing projects, from poor families and from wealthy ones, young men have come together to play football for Auburn.

Their stories have been as varied as their backgrounds. They've overcome daunting challenges on and off the field. They've celebrated great victories, and wept in the wake of painful defeats.

Who better to tell those stories than Rob Pate, who lived the Auburn football experience in his unique way? Rob was a hard-nosed, hard-playing football player on the field, and a deep thinker off the field. It comes as no surprise to anyone who knows him that he has gone on to be successful in his life.

Rob knows what it takes to play college football at the highest level, and to succeed in school. He knows about looking into the face of adversity and refusing to blink. He's been there.

INTRODUCTION

The Role of Athletics in Future Success

My entire life has been shaped by organized athletics. There is no denying the lessons learned in competition on playing surfaces as a child, adolescent, teenager, and young adult were life-altering in a positive way. The attributes of teamwork, discipline, reliability, humility, sportsmanship, and perseverance flooded over into all facets of my life, and formed a foundation for the person I would become. The education I received through sports is the backbone of who I am, and there is not a day that passes I'm not immensely grateful for the coaches, teammates, and support personnel who had a hand in pushing me to achieve successes I could never realize on my own. There is not a day that passes I do not draw from lessons learned or benefit from behaviors adopted in athletics.

Athletics are special, and if properly trained, encouraged, and cultivated, the product bred will undoubtedly be a finer finished creation. It may sound easy. It may seem that any half-hearted effort on a soccer field or baseball diamond or basketball court would be the impetus for a positive force in one's life. Perhaps it could be. But, in reality, the truth is it takes a commitment from all involved to make athletics that exceptional, unique driving force for the individual. Early on, the triad of parents, coaches, and player working in tandem toward a common goal is absolutely necessary to see growth in the athlete. One leg not holding its own can potentially cause systematic failure and negate the intended outcome. That triad is crucial.

There is something extraordinary about becoming a part of something much greater than yourself. In today's selfish, materialistic, all-about-me world, learning to take a back seat for the betterment of the team is a hard lesson. It goes against our natural instincts, our natural inclination to look out for ourselves as rule number one. Team sports quickly eliminate this mind-set, because teams filled with selfish personalities are unsuccessful teams. Rather, it's the teams that sacrifice for one another, love each other, respect the abilities of their teammates, are coachable, communicate well, work to improve each day—these are teams that become champions. These are the athletes who become great spouses, become great employees, become great people.

Though individual sports contain many of the same elements that allow personal growth on and off the playing surface, it is team sports that I believe most eloquently represent real-world challenges and opportunities to enhance one's response to them. Team sports require trust, reliance, accountability, communication, empathy, and synergy. The whole is greater than of the sum of its parts. The team takes priority over self, yet individuals comprising the team must wholly buy into the concept or the team sinks. It's a microcosm of life in the real world. It's a training ground for leadership and experience in handling life's challenges. It's a mechanism to enhance character and mold minds to be tougher. It's a world of sacrifice in exchange for a greater reward of accomplishment. It's a fertile ground of growth and maturity in more ways than can be imagined.

I understand that athletics are not meant to be played by everyone. Some may be limited with handicaps, others may have other passions far away from a football field—in a science lab, on a stage, or with an instrument. I contend, however, that the principles still hold. The values essential to athletic achievement are no different from those that bring artistic acclaim. Therefore, no matter where your passions lie, whatever your field of work, or why you chose to pick up this book and read this far, the ideals obtained through athletics can push us all, directly or indirectly, toward success in numerous areas of our lives. Athletics is an art form, the athlete the canvas, growth and maturity the finished work—building blocks forever ingrained.

CHAPTER ONE

Principle of Hard Work

"Work! Hard work!" This was the slogan we ended every single workout or conditioning session we had when Coach Kevin Yoxall became Auburn's strength and conditioning coach prior to the 1999 season at Auburn University. It wasn't a saying generated by the players; it was created and demanded by Coach Yox. It was both a reminder and a challenge daily to remember why we were a 3-8 football team and what would be required to not only compete but to excel in the most difficult league in college football. Nothing would be given. Nothing would come easily. If we as a team and as individuals wanted to taste success and victory, a heavy price would have to be paid under the direction of Coach Yox. It would be "Work! Hard work!" And we hated it. But we loved him for it. Because he was right and the results were obvious.

Over a decade of Auburn players were molded into tougher men by Coach Kevin Yoxall. As he exited the Auburn program, having served it in an elite manner for fourteen years, there was a generation of former and current Auburn players who felt a piece of them exit with Coach Yox.

And I was there to see the transformation he ushered in. I was there the night Coach Tuberville told us in a team meeting that he was hiring a strength coach who could and would physically throw us out of the weight room if he deemed it necessary. I was there the night we performed our very first conditioning regimen under Coach Yox—a measly three gassers inside the indoor complex. It was the least amount of running we'd ever do for him, and we had more players than you could imagine who failed the test. I was there to see many teammates walk out and never return. And I was there to see us go from a 3-8 team to an SEC Championship game after only two years under a work ethic he installed.

Before Coach Yox came to Auburn, we were incredibly weak in mind and body. He blew us away with his structure, intensity, demands, expertise, and his passion. I believe I can safely speak on behalf of my teammates, and all those who've followed, in saying that Kevin Yoxall positively impacted our lives for the better, forced us to grow up, and demanded excellence every single day. He shaped the way we now think, work, respond, and raise our children.

We hated his guts initially. Cussed him within the confines and anonymity of our lockerroom. Would have bet my life he conferred with Satan himself to create daily workouts. Dreaded each day during class, wondering what torturous running he had planned, what awkward lift he would stand and observe me perform. There was no guessing, no cheating, no way to coast through a workout. He, or one of his GAs, watched every rep of every exercise of every individual who entered the weight room. He had even prepopulated the weight to be placed on the bar for each lift, using an algorithm to be certain he could track our progress to see who was producing and who wasn't.

He made us dress exactly the same: Auburn-issued orange shorts with Auburn-issued gray T-shirt. You wore something different, you wished you hadn't. You showed up late, not five minutes, but one second, you wished you hadn't.

As we began to see the results of our hard work, a work ethic we all thought we epitomized prior to Coach Yox's arrival—but a work ethic we actually hadn't come close to obtaining—we began to buy in. It became crystal clear that there was no easy path to success, that "work, hard work" was the price to pay to reap rewards. It was also evident to the players the effort and desire Coach Yox put into his own daily grind. He was the hardest working coach on staff, hands down.

Yes, he was building us into leaner, faster, stronger versions of ourselves. But he was also laying the foundation for each of us to live successful lives. He was equipping us with mental toughness, with overcoming seemingly insurmountable circumstances—with what it meant to be held accountable, and with the understanding that to be and beat the best, no matter what the task, you must outwork, outcompete, outlast the best. He was the catalyst who resurrected a program from the ashes to national preeminence.

The longer we were around him the more we appreciated him. We understood the reasoning behind the hellish routine and grew to expect it, to persevere, and to be better off because of the effort. In the moment, he was a bastard sent straight to Auburn from the pit of hell. In the aftermath, he was a father figure, a mentor, a leader, the master—the best there is or was.

Ask any football player who was at Auburn from 1999 to 2012, and 99.9 percent of them will tell you Yox was the most influential and respected coach they had during their careers. More so than the head coach. More so than the coach who recruited them to campus. More so than their position coach. We all spent infinitely more time with Yox than all of the above combined. He coddled no one. He played favorites to no one. He loved us all the same, and we never questioned his commitment to us.

After the 2010 national title victory, I wrote the following on my blog:

> *"My biggest behind-the-scenes contributors were the two men who were brought to campus by Coach Tuberville, and who have been the most instrumental hires Auburn University has made in its athletic department bar none ... to you Coach Yox and Chette Williams ... you're like fathers to us players; you mold us physically and spiritually into men by pushing us beyond our comfort zones; you make us believe in our abilities and in each other by the work ethic you instill, the ear you lend, the encouragement you provide. You are the best in the business at what you both do and Auburn is lucky to have you. You both deserve this more than anyone else associated with Auburn athletics, and I for one am grateful for what you meant to not only this team, but what you have meant to my life! Thank you!"*

In my view, Coach Yox left a legacy at Auburn University that will live on as long as any of us who played under his tenure are breathing air. We'll all forever be indebted to Yox for forcing us to push beyond our comfort zones, down deep into a core existence we never knew we were capable of achieving. He brought out the best in us. He demanded it every day. I'm a better husband, father, optometrist, person, because of the lessons I took with me from Auburn. Many of those lessons came from Kevin Yoxall.

Ultimately, what was learned from my time with Coach Yoxall is what makes participation in athletics worthwhile. To reach your potential, and move far beyond the limits you've erected in your psyche, will require you to work harder than you dare dream possible. To achieve progress and growth in not only your skill set, but more importantly in your mentality and belief system, will require you to walk through hell to hone your abilities. If something comes easily without hard work, discipline, and sacrifice, then chances are you are not maximizing your talents and gifts. This lesson was taught daily by Coach Yox. I'm forever grateful.

There are not enough positive adjectives I can use to convey even a fraction of the wisdom, skills and toughness Coach Kevin Yoxall has imparted to young men from coast to coast. He is simply the best at his trade. Till the day I die, the mention of "hard work" will always equate to Coach Yox—a father figure to many, providing the discipline and structure that has impacted all of our lives far beyond our time with him.

Biography

Kevin Yoxall assumed duties as Rice's head strength and conditioning coach in January 2014.

A veteran of twenty-six years on the collegiate level, Yoxall comes to Rice after spending one year supervising the strength and conditioning programs at Strake Jesuit School in Houston. Prior to Strake, Yoxall was the head strength and conditioning coach at Auburn for fourteen years.

Yoxall earned his undergraduate degree from East Texas State and began his coaching career in 1987 at TCU as a graduate assistant. Two years later, after earning his master's in physical education, he was promoted to the head strength coaching position with the Horned Frogs. He left Fort Worth in 1992 to take over the conditioning programs at Minnesota, then moved west in 1996 to guide the strength and conditioning program at UCLA before moving on to Auburn in January of 1999.

Yoxall set a collegiate regional record for power lifting in 1982, and was named a Collegiate All-American power lifter in 1983. He was named Collegiate Strength and Conditioning Coach of the Year by the Professional Football Strength and Conditioning Coaches Society in 2005, and the Pac-10 Strength and Conditioning Coach of the Year in 1998. Yoxall received his profession's highest honor in 2002, when the Collegiate Strength and Conditioning Coaches Association named him "Master Strength and Conditioning Coach."

He and his wife, Nancy, have two children, Collin and Marlee.[1]

---

[1]www.riceowls.com

Toughness and Work Ethic in Sport

By Coach Kevin Yoxall

Throughout my career as a collegiate strength and conditioning coach, I've been asked many times about the toughness of athletes, and who were some of the toughest athletes that I coached. I have always felt that the athletes who fell into the category of great overall toughness were not necessarily the ones who lifted the heaviest weight, or for the most reps, nor were the fastest runners. In my mind, the toughest athletes I have had the privilege to train over the years are those women *and* men who show complete dedication to the task at hand for that particular day's training, no matter how difficult the workout was going to be.

These athletes are consistent in their approach to a training day, no matter how good or bad they feel physically or mentally. The toughest athletes *always* come to train with the attitude that, for the next hour or two or three, they are training for positive results and success, which will be reflected in the results when they actually compete in their sport. The toughest athletes do not simply show up for a training session with an attitude of "Well, we have to be here, we might as well get it done." The focus of the toughest athletes I've encountered always is superior to others who want to just simply get in, train, and get out. The athletes in this group include those who are vocal, and others who never say a word but still are noticed by their teammates for their "tunnel vision" approach to train hard, and with a mind-set to accomplish all the tasks for that session successfully.

The toughest athletes are the ones who never show that he or she is defeated in a workout session. They go the extra yardage than the distance called for in a conditioning rep, and don't look at doing something like that as special. In their minds it's what you *should* do in order to continue to get better for competition. The toughest athletes I've coached over the years are special, and it's always my pleasure to encounter those women and men. It would be impossible to name any of them for fear of leaving someone off that list who certainly deserves to be included. It would, however, be safe to say that if I did make a list of the toughest athletes I've had the privilege to train, they would all be very humble about being included in that group. To train hard day in and day out for these athletes was, and is, a part of what a great competitor is supposed to do.

CHAPTER TWO

Selfless Values in a Selfish Society

We receive conflicting messages in sports. At a young age you're taught to be viciously competitive, hammer the opposition, take no prisoners on the field of play. Contrastingly, you're taught sportsmanship, in which you help your opponent to his feet, respect the abilities of the guy lined up opposite you, pray together at the conclusion of your battle.

You're told to have fun, enjoy your sport, but also that the fun is in the winning. You're told to be a team player, there is no "I" in team, no one individual is greater than the collective team; yet you're inundated with advertising, *SportsCenter*, and athletes deemed the greatest in their sport, which is the antithesis of being team oriented. The message and necessity of leadership is bantered about in every locker room, on every team, urging guys to step into that crucial role. Some do so by example, others verbally. Often the message is mixed: "too many chiefs, not enough Indians" produces problems In that it becomes a confusing world for the young athlete, yet these messages shape the demeanor and thought process of those on the receiving end.

The media, thereby much of society, hears little of the model teammate making disciplined choices on and off the playing field that benefits his team. The grunt who solidifies a unit with the toughness, maturity, and levelheadedness all teams must have to reach the pinnacle is barely noticed by today's media, nor, as a result, by fans of the game. A teammate with more talent but who is irreverent, all about himself, coarse and a diva on and off the court? We give him shoe contracts, interviews on major networks, glorified for glorifying himself. It's a tough sale to today's youngsters. They know what they see. They struggle with this contradiction. We all do.

In life, the business world—it's no different. In an increasingly "all about me" materialistic society, we all struggle with the clash of fighting for ourselves (me) versus fighting for *us* (team, employer, community, family). Being the friend or coworker you desire in your friends and coworkers, rather than being the friend or coworker who is looking out for number one. Sometimes those are mutually inclusive; often they are in opposition. I believe former and current athletes are at a unique advantage in this climate because they've been exposed to this environment often, and are forced to overcome it in order to be a success in their sport.

We celebrate diversity in this country for good reason. We all learn from other cultures, from differences in people, from different viewpoints. Athletics lays the foundation for this mindset. Many of my teammates did not look like me. We came from very diverse backgrounds, had different off the field interests, were dissimilar in many more ways. This wasn't a barrier for us; rather, this was appealing, interesting, and entertaining. We were able to set aside the dividing lines society had drawn around us, and instead work together for a common goal. Every team I played on was like this. Whether it be race, wealth, religion, sexuality—all the problems this world divides over, we never had a second thought about. That's a beautiful thing. And that's the advantage athletics brings to the individual.

Think for a moment about the disunion of our nation, particularly the political division we see daily. Red versus blue. Black versus white. Old versus young. Male versus female. Gay versus straight. Liberal versus conservative. Seldom do we see agreement in today's world of politics. Each side is pitted against the other in a game of mutual destruction. Tear each other down. We see fighting to win rather than fighting for what's right. We see groups fight for self-interests rather than wage war for the good of society. Selfishness. Power. Greed. These are the core tenets of political life in America.

You show me a team with these destructive core values, and I'll show you a team with more losses than victories. You show me a person driven and filled with these attributes, and I'll show you an individual who is unhappy when alone in his quiet moments. In team sports, athletes are forced to sacrifice selfishness for altruism, power for cohesion, greed for generosity. Good teams have leadership that preaches this. Those individuals who buy in and apply it to their lives enjoy successes and happiness. It's simple yet incredibly complex and difficult to attain, because it collides head-on with societal norms. But, as I said, societal norms have a way of being overcome in locker rooms all over this country. Sports is the catalyst, the athlete the beneficiary, of lessons taught by becoming something much greater than yourself.

Athletics teaches selfless values to kids being raised in a selfish society. Athletes are among the very first to see the true value in selflessness by virtue of team sports. Giving up your body for the ground ball to prevent the double play; to take on the pulling guard; to take the charge; to open a hole allowing a teammate to gain extra rushing yards. These traits do not arise from nothing. Such characteristics are fostered and nurtured by coaches and team leaders elevating the team above the individual. Sacrifice for the success of the team becomes sacrificing for the good of the corporation, family, church, country, community. Learning to be selfless is perhaps the greatest attribute team sports has to offer.

Randy Overstreet was my pastor at Double Oak Community Church, a church he founded in Birmingham, Alabama, in 2005. Double Oak Community Church has thrived, thanks to Randy's vision. He stepped down as pastor of Double Oak in 2012, feeling called to revive dying or challenged churches in the Birmingham area by serving as an interim pastor, while also providing financial advice towards debt elimination and restructuring. He is a jokester, a comic, a pastor who knows and loves his congregation, a spiritual leader, a friend to many.

Biography

Randy Overstreet was the founding pastor of Double Oak Community Church in Mt. Laurel, Alabama. Rev. Overstreet grew up in Birmingham and graduated from Samford University and Grace Seminary. His commitment to preaching God's word, his quick wit and dynamic sense of humor has made Randy a very popular conference and retreat speaker. He has been in the ministry for twenty-five years and, after sensing God's call for him to plant a church, he did so in the Mt. Laurel community. On Easter Sunday, 2005, he started Double Oak Community Church (DOCC) with ten people.[1] Four years later, DOCC has an attendance of over seven hundred. God has gifted Randy with an excellent ability to effectively communicate the truths of God's word to His people. Randy and his wife, Sandra, have been married for twenty-five years and have two children.

---

[1]www.doubleoakcc.org

Biblical Winning, Leading, and Competing

By Randy Overstreet

Winning I

"An athlete is not crowned unless he competes according to the rules" ... "Run with endurance the race set before you" ... "All run but only one wins the prize" ... "I've fought the good fight, I've finished the course!" These are not quotes from a coach or a teammate trying to motivate his team to win a game or prepare his team for competition. This is the Word of God preparing me for life!

I enjoy everything about sports. Watching, playing and coaching. Sports has been a big part of my life for almost a half century. In fact, at the time I am writing this I am competing in a three-day golf tournament. Growing up in an athletic family, sports and competition were how our family spent time with each other. If you could bounce it, throw it or catch it, I was playing it. Sports not only taught me how to play a particular game, sports taught me about life. In leading a congregation, I've had to keep in check my love to compete and win! Before my son was born I prayed for a safe delivery, then added "Lord, if he grows up to be 6' 4", runs a 4.2 forty-yard dash and has hands like fly paper, I'll give you the Glory!" I told you I was competitive! (Kidding, of course.) A level-headed, wisdom-soaked wife help put things in perspective. "It's a game. Enjoy it, learn from it, and use it as an opportunity to invest quality time in my son both spiritually and athletically."

As a pastor, there are some good applications that I have learned from my days as an athlete.

Leading

As a pastor, I have found that being a former athlete really is an advantage when it comes to relating and leading men in the congregation. It helps because we live in a culture where commercials, sitcoms, and movies are being used to make men look weak, stupid and foolish. That's why I meet with small groups of men regularly. I want to model Biblical manhood before them. That doesn't mean displaying a macho camacho attitude all the time. Real men cry, hurt, and are transparent enough to say, "I don't have it together all the time." Men need accountability, so a lot of times I lead one on one. Much is accomplished that way. *"As iron sharpens iron, so one man sharpens another"* (Proverbs 27:17).

In sports, coaches break the team down into offense, defense, and special teams, placing each individual where he fits best. As a pastor, I've learned to do the same. I hired my staff that were trained and gifted in their ministry areas. As new members come into the church, we line them up in a ministry according to their gifts and talents. I remember as a freshman in high school, fifteen guys tried out for quarterback, including a 5'7" 300-pounder. The coach quickly deduced who was QB material and placed everyone where they could help the team. As we lead in the church, we must likewise place those according to their giftedness.

The greatest joy I have, however, is investing in my staff. I now have student pastors who are senior pastors. I get great joy in seeing them grow in their work and ministry. Part of leading is always growing your staff to one day lead. How many college coaches started as assistants under the likes of Bear Bryant, Bobby Bowden, and John Wooden? These men invested in others and, thereby, launched them into being leaders of their own. I feel the same obligation.

Competing

There is *big time competition* with pastoring. The competition is not with other pastors and churches, but with Satan himself. He is a relentless opponent. The Bible in fact uses athletic language as it says, *"We wrestle with this evil dark force"* (Eph 6:12). To put it simply, Satan wants to destroy lives. I preach the gospel and partner as a reconciler with God, so that people may be transformed for eternity. I'm always looking for opportunity to step into the flow of others' lives to get leverage and earn a right to be heard. I remind myself that in order to win a right to be heard, I must "walk in a manner worthy of the Gospel" (Phil 1:27).

Competing with others' opinions and ideas in the congregation is another example. Everybody wants his or her way! "We need to do it like the church down the street." Situations that require church discipline can cause people to rebel. Sometimes leadership means looking them in the eye and saying tough things in love (Gal 6:1).

Winning II

Everybody likes winning. I like to win. I would do anything for a trophy as a kid. As I have matured over the years, I have found that one of the biggest competitors I have is myself. You see great athletes accomplish great feats and do unbelievable things on the field and court, but tnot be able to manage their lives off the field. The news is filled with broken relationships, and all types of addiction of college and professional athletes. It's amazing how small things, such as what comes out of grapes and coco leaves, can defeat a man. Recent stories involving Ray Rice and Dustin Johnson are only the tip of the iceberg. You see, we as Christ followers still have an old nature. This nature wants and demands its way. My new nature in Christ. however, says no way to the old way! I have to remind myself that I'm no longer obligated to feed my old nature, because of the crucified and risen Christ who lives in me in the person of the Holy Spirit.

Guaranteed Victory

Joe Namath, on the eve of the Super Bowl, once "guaranteed victory" before the game was played. He actually delivered!

No coach or player in his right mind should do that. In a day of parody, one should be careful. Both players and coaches have eaten crow by prematurely claiming victory.

My father-in-law was an interesting man. He enjoyed wagering on horse races, but didn't want to lose his hard-earned money. Since there wasn't a race track near his house, he would invite friends over to watch the races. Confidently, he would engage in friendly wagers with the guys. The friends were always amazed at my father-in-law's ability to pick a winner. One day he told me the secret to his success. He would video record the race to show his friends after he had already watched the end! I miss that guy. One stark difference between sports and ministry is that I can honestly declare a guaranteed victory. Not because of any effort of my own or anything I can do; it's because of what Jesus Christ did on the cross. As I live life, I live in and fight *from* victory ... not *for* victory. My competition is doomed because Christ has conquered sin, death, the grave and Satan. In a day of life coaches and self help Gurus, change, help and guaranteed victory can only be found in a Savior: Jesus Christ. *"Death is swallowed up in victory. O death where is your victory? O death where is your sting?*

The sting of death is sin, and the power of sin is the law. But thanks be to God who gives us the victory through Jesus Christ our Lord!" (1 Cor 15:54-56).

Verses at the beginning
2 Tim 2:5
Heb 12:1b
1 Cor 9:24
2 Tim 4:7
All verses from the ESV version

CHAPTER THREE

Discipline

Discipline is a powerful force. It wakes you from a peaceful sleep in a warm bed to hit the street before sunrise for a long run *(Runners sicken me!)*. Discipline prompts you to make tough choices in the interim that result in triumph in the end. It's the motivation that pushes us beyond what's comfortable. It's the impetus for driving us to out-work, out-hustle, outplan our competition. Successful athletes have essentially placed discipline as the puppeteer, pulling the strings of the athletes' decision-making tree. Should I do more/less of this? Discipline provides the answer and sets the course. Can I push myself beyond what I previously thought was possible? Discipline provides the fortitude to make it happen. Not every person is disciplined. Not every athlete bows to its demands. But the most accomplished athletes are far and away the most disciplined.

Discipline extends far beyond the athletic playing surfaces for the talented athlete. His success on the field of play comes from discipline exerted away from the game. The late Junior

Seau was the most gifted, passionate, smart football player with whom I ever had the pleasure of sharing a huddle. He had an uncanny ability to recognize offensive pre-nap alignment, and then make adjustments before the ball was snapped. For instance, he could tell by observing an offensive lineman in his stance whether he would be run- or pass-blocking. He would change our defensive assignments based on his intuition. That insight did not just happen by osmosis. It emerged from years of study and attention to detail, both on and off the field.

Many intuitive, clever lay people could study film, pick up tendencies, and utilize the information to create an advantage before the ball is snapped. But what happens when the ball is snapped? That depends on how disciplined the player has been in many areas. Weight room, nutrition, practice, film study, preparation—all become factors when the ball is put into play. That's where we see separation between people. Not many lay people are willing to put in the sacrifice it takes to be that player. Game days appear glorious; the athlete is the star. Little thought is put into what the athlete endured in the offseason to make it on game day. I tried to make it a mission in my book, *A Tiger's Walk: Memoirs of an Auburn Football Player*. It was obvious to me that the general public had little idea what collegiate athletes bore on a daily basis. I wanted to shed light on it, even if it was but a single ray, because if the price to pay to play at that level was costly, it needed to be recognized. Why? It boils down to discipline.

Whether your sport is football or golf, gymnastics or lacrosse, success ultimately resides in the hands of discipline. An average athlete with impeccable discipline will succeed by a far greater proportion than an elite athlete with abysmal discipline. Discipline is not the only ingredient needed to achieve athletic achievement, but it is undoubtedly the necessary backbone or foundation to build upon.

There is no question but that participation in athletics at an early age taught me this valuable lesson out of the gate. It wasn't lost on me as a youngster that hard work was no fun, but ultimately you reap what you sow. Hard work was difficult, but not as difficult as walking off the field the loser. In today's "everybody wins, let's give everyone a trophy" mentality that seems to have infiltrated athletics at this critical developmental age, kids are not learning the principal of reaping what is sown. Instead, they're being rewarded for mediocrity, rewarded regardless of effort. That's a dangerous slope in my view. I realize there are more pressing issues in the growth and development of children, but learning to be disciplined doesn't just magically occur. And lack of discipline in the make-up of the child puts him or her at an immense disadvantage moving forward.

For me, the discipline gained on the athletic field translated to discipline in the classroom, discipline in time management, and discipline in relationships. There's no guarantee all athletes prosper equally in this manner, but each has the opportunity to transfer athletic lessons into personal accomplishment. It was likely the single greatest message I received from sports, and undeniably assisted in molding me into the person I became.

Did I enjoy practicing football in the Alabama August heat? No. Did I relish coaches chiding excellence out of me as an elementary kid? Not really. Did I look forward to mat drills, conditioning tests, suicides, foul poles? No, no, no, and hell no. I hated all of them. But I also didn't look forward to a challenging Auburn curriculum, or professional school at UAB, or working through difficult issues with my wife or children or employees. Without the background of athletics, I seriously question the manner in which I would have responded to life challenges. Athletics taught perseverance. Athletics taught communication. Athletics taught respecting the opposition. It taught me to dig deeper than I thought I was capable of. To rise to the occasion when called upon. It taught the reap and sow principle. And for that I will forever be indebted to my athletic upbringing.

Coach Phillip Lolley was my position coach during my junior and senior seasons at Auburn University. I always admired Coach Lolley's knowledge of the game, but truly appreciated his player-centric, positive approach. He was the picture of discipline in his study, his work ethic, his physical well-being (it wasn't odd to walk into the weight room and see Coach bench pressing 315 pounds without a spot multiple times), and his skill at building trusting relationships with his players. His time at Auburn saw him serve in many disparate roles, all of which he handled with precision, class, wisdom, and hunger to succeed. He is football to his core. He cannot have a conversation with you without football dominating the discussion. It's in his blood. It's who he is. And Auburn University and the student athletes he mentored are better off because of Coach Phillip Lolley.

Biography

A member of the Auburn family since 1999, Phillip Lolley spent seven seasons as Auburn's defensive backs coach under Tommy Tuberville (2000-03) and Gene Chizik (2009-11); among his top pupils were Jim Thorpe Award winner Carlo Rogers and Junior Rosegreen, both Auburn All-Americans.

Lolley joined the Tigers in 1999 as a strength and conditioning coach, and was AU's Director of NFL Relations from 2004-08. A twenty-two-year veteran high school coach in the state of Alabama, Lolley was head coach at three schools: North Jackson (winning the 1993 4A state championship) from 1988-98; South Choctaw Academy in 1977; and Warrior Academy in Eutaw, from 1978-82. He also served as defensive coordinator at Demopolis High School (1982-84) and head coach at Stevenson High School (1984-87).[1]

---

[1]www.auburntigers.com

Discipline

By Phillip Lolley

What is the definition of a disciplined football team?

An extremely disciplined team must pay attention to what it needs to do, no matter how hard it gets. If someone makes a mistake, he is accountable, period.

Building that accountability does not come easily, but that's okay. If it's easy, you don't learn anything from it.

There's discipline for failure to adhere to the rules set forth by the team, and there's also discipline in building your team to its fullest capability.

In my view as a coach, discipline was not a recreation; it was a punishment.

And my rule was, it must be fair but hard.

They would be punished fairly, but they would be accountable for their actions. To have discipline, you have to teach it, you have to coach it and not allow them to do anything other than what is expected.

When they don't do what you want, there has to be something that makes them want to follow the rules. The punishment has to be fair, but also it has to be a deterrent to repeat actions. Actions that can be on-field mistakes or penalties, not going to class, something at night, or breaking team rules of any kind.

When you are being disciplined, whatever I ask you to do will be hard, because I don't want you to do this again.

Discipline equates to structure. When you show kids you are doing something to make them better, they want that structure. You have to hold them to what you want and not turn your back. You have to be consistent, every day.

If you set a rule and say, "This is it, no way out," then you have to back up what you say. You can't bend. And you can't have eight or nine assistant coaches doing discipline their own way, because people by nature are different and one coach might go easier than another. That's not a team, and that's not fair to your guys. Everyone must be on the same page. We must be one and become one.

Whatever is expected, there is a form of structure to those expectations and they must be achievable. There's a difference between discipline aimed toward something you're capable of doing, as opposed to discipline that asks more than someone is capable of achieving. You should never punish a team for what they're not capable of doing—ever.

You get what you want out of discipline by what you put in.

And the attitude of a disciplined team becomes a point of pride with all its members. In high school, I would select to serve as leaders a group of players who had earned the respect of the team. I would allow the team to help select those leaders. Then I asked the leaders of the team to set up rules and guidelines. The players knew it was not a dictatorship; it was a team endeavor incorporating their ideas.

If we had a situation that went against our rules, I would ask those leaders, "What do you think should be the punishment?" The players were often harder than I would have been about that punishment and the team policies. But they wanted accountability.

Your players, and those in your program, will never forget the lessons you teach them if you are sincere about what you want from them and for them as a team.

My own high school coach, William Elmore, was a man I respected and loved. I knew he cared about me, and that he was going to hold me accountable for my actions. He expected a lot from me because he considered me a leader, and I was not going to let him down.

In 1997 his wife, Opal, called me from the hospital and said he was dying. I got in the car immediately; I loved that man. He was tough on us but we loved him and we didn't want to let him down. Anything he asked me to do, I would do it no matter how tough, because I knew he cared. To me, he was an example of how to build a disciplined team.

One philosophy I've always found to be true: you can be hard on them, but if you take a dime from them give them a nickel back. Encourage them after you've made a correction.

You are building men for life, and you can't take shortcuts or they will fail when things get toughest.

CHAPTER FOUR

Letting Go of Mistakes—Having Short Memories

Mistakes are a part of athletic life. Great effort is taken to minimize mistakes in competition, as well as to take advantage of the slipups of your opponent. If a pitcher hangs a curve ball belt high he holds his breath, as the miscue gives the batter the opportunity to capitalize mercilessly. When the quarterback fires the ball across the middle of a defense into a window that existed before his release but closed as the ball left his hand, momentum shifts in an instant. The catcher who has the baserunner nailed stealing third base, only to sail the ball into left field must watch the runner score on his error. They are common mistakes that hurt the team and sting the player committing the fault. Momentary failure has occurred; how do you respond?

All sports give the athlete ample opportunity to respond to these challenges. We all make mistakes, sometimes at devastatingly key moments in crucial contests. Can we put it behind us and move on from the miscue, or does it eat away at our confidence and our will to compete, allowing one mistake to escalate to the point where it threatens to defeat us more than once? A great athlete plays with a free conscience and an understanding that mistakes do not define him as a player. Mistakes are inevitable, but they certainly do not have to dominate our thoughts and paralyze our instincts. Great athletes have learned to accept gaffes and screw-ups as part of what comes with the territory, yet refuse to allow potential pitfalls to reduce their drive or slow down the speed or aggression with which they play.

As a former defensive back, I am certainly partial to the defensive side of the football. In my view, rules in football are constantly in flux, attempting to give every advantage possible to the offensive units. Defensive backs find themselves on islands with little tactical advantage to defend against high-powered, vertically oriented offenses. The rules against physically challenging receivers across the football field force corners in the NFL to be the best athletes in the world. They must run stride for stride with elite wideouts, most of whom tower over them. They must defend the most precise routes with the ball arriving with stunning accuracy at speeds beyond our comprehension. They can't touch the receiver, or even give the appearance of touching the receiver, lest they draw a costly pass interference penalty. They must contend with avoiding contact with a "defenseless" receiver, and have tnow even lost the ability to jar the ball loose with a vicious hit in the name of player safety (never mind a "defenseless" defender being blindsided by an offensive player, as defenders are rarely protected under the rule book). Needless to say, their job is absurdly difficult.

Even so, many corners in the NFL remain exceptionally successful at their craft. They develop a sort of sixth sense of anticipation, and befuddle offenses with heady play combined with off-the-charts athleticism. They outleap and win the physical battles against receivers who are often a head taller and many pounds heavier than they are. But even the greatest among them have failure rates much higher than surrounding teammates playing other positions. With more challenges come more opportunities to fail, and these superior athletes fail quite often. There are not many low scoring defensive slugfest football games these days, because offenses attack ruthlessly. And, ironically, the "failures" in this offensive age of football are laid at the feet of the defensive backs—the greatest athletes in the world.

What separates the greatest cornerbacks in the game from the others is their ability to forget their mistakes, compartmentalize opponents' successes at their expense, and fight for four quarters as if they own the football field. They become masters of having short memories. It's an amazingly trying mental hurdle, yet the ones who accomplish the feat are the ones who garner the most success. It takes a special person who believes wholly in his talents to continually fail yet retain his greatness.

Golf is another example of a sport that toys with the mental capacity of the golfer to put the bad behind him, or else have the past ruin the present and the future. The lesser caliber golfer hits a ball poorly after several holes of quality consistency then begins questioning every nuanced detail of his grip, backswing, club face, and wind. Though he has connected with precision on the overwhelming majority of his swings, it is the single failure that controls his thoughts and now threatens to torpedo his score. He simply cannot get the shank out of his mind, leading to shank after shank. I am that golfer.

The professional golfer, however, stares down a hole and knows exactly his plan of attack, visualizing each shot before he executes that vision. His mind isn't filled with doubt or dread of a poor swing, but rather is fully confident he has practiced his skill to perfection and will now unleash his brilliance. Though every shot does not fall as he has envisioned, he is not disturbed and conquered by his lack of execution. Instead, he is confident in his ability to overcome his newfound lie. No predicament is too high an obstacle; he has trained for every conceivable shot on the golf course. He can forget his mistakes because he knows new opportunities are in store immediately. He has mastered the short memory and it makes all the difference in the world.

Sports teaches the valuable lesson of failure, and the corresponding message of moving beyond the mistakes that lead to loss. When that message sinks in within the realm of athletics it can then be transferred with ease to life. Struggles that arrive at points in life, or even adversities that become permanent scars, do not have to become our identity nor define us as individuals. Challenges we seek to solve, yet sometimes fall short of the mark, can become opportunities for growth and improvement, as opposed to areas of anger or resentment. Sports teaches you to live to see the next battle, and to learn from your blunders, as opposed to wallowing in them. Far worse than a mistake giving rise to failure is for that mistake to perpetuate future failures because of the inability to move beyond the initial misfire. Mistakes may forever be a part of anything we try that is worthwhile, but perfecting the art of the short memory aids in keeping us striving to improve what we have begun.

Travaris Robinson: An Example in Forgetting Failures

This article was published on AuburnUndercover.com on January 7, 2015. Travaris Robinson (T-Rob) was a teammate of mine who arrived my junior year at Auburn. He unselfishly played numerous positions at Auburn striving for excellence and the betterment of our team. At the conclusion of his NFL career, T-Rob transitioned immediately into coaching and quickly rose to become one of the nation's most coveted teachers and recruiters in college football.

T-Rob Earned Respect

With the addition of Travaris Robinson to Gus Malzhan's coaching staff, I now have two former teammates manning the sideline for the Auburn Tigers. Dameyune Craig was a senior quarterback my freshman year—our emotional leader, our offensive hope, passing our team to ten wins and one point shy of a conference title. T-Rob was a freshman my junior year, arriving as a part of Tommy Tuberville's inaugural Auburn class from Miami as a slot receiver. It did not take Travaris long to see action on the field, earning immediate playing time as a possession receiver, a dedicated blocker, a guy willing and able to serve many functions as a utility type player.

Recruiting when I played was so far removed from what we see today it's hardly recognizable. Guys today know each other long before they become teammates on the Plains. They are connected by cell phones, social media, websites such as *AuburnUndercover*, national All-Star games, and several additional camps and on-campus events that bring them together. I may have met a handful of my future teammates on my official visit, a few more in the Alabama-Mississippi All-Star game, but that was it. We didn't know beforehand many players on the team, many players in our class, or who our coaches were even recruiting to fill out our class.

Guys like T-Rob made the experience of learning to adapt, fit, mesh with your teammate an easy and enjoyable task. He earned the respect of us all with his work ethic, his willingness to disregard his stature and mix it up with defenders twice his size, his sure hands, his playmaking ability. He was a guy likeable enough to converse effortlessly with the upperclassmen just as easily as with his signing class. His personality was the perfect combination of jesting fun if the environment was suitable, or focused concentration and seriousness when warranted.

Regardless of circumstance, you knew T-Rob would give maximum effort and pull his weight. He was the type of teammate you loved going to war with. The type of teammate you'd want in your corner in a dark alley, as well as by your side at your wedding. There aren't a ton of T-Robs out there.

What stands out most to me about my time with him was his unselfishness. He could have been a prolific wide receiver, there's not a doubt in my mind. As a true freshman his number was called upon often to move the chains; he became one of QB Ben Leard's favorite targets in 1999. After beginning his sophomore season serving that same role, he was moved to my group to play corner and supply depth to a much needed position. His first game action at corner he was atrocious, almost singlehandedly allowing Northern Illinois to come back and make a blowout game palatable by giving up two long touchdown passes. He was picked on in that game, and his newness in the position was obvious. He didn't complain, ask to return to his WR position, or change his joyful exuberance at all. He kept working, kept improving, kept learning, kept on being a teammate you respect and love.

As I former left and, he became a safety for a new defensive coordinator named Gene Chizik, and his athletic ability, football savvy, and leadership qualities flourished, making him into an All-Conference player. For guys like me who saw young DBs like T-Rob and Roderick Hood become elite playmakers in the Southeastern Conference, it came as no surprise. More than the athletic ability, it was the mental makeup, the desire to improve, the fearlessness, and drive to compete that told me all I needed to know. T-Rob was a winner and we all knew it.

As Travaris has entered the coaching ranks, he has attacked the profession just as he did the opportunity to be a student athlete. It was only a matter of time before his value skyrocketed. The University of Florida has been the beneficiary of his stellar recruiting capabilities that stem from his work ethic, his ability to relate to the guys he recruits both athletically and socially, his ability to connect with young men like few others can. The fact that Coach Muschamp believes in T-Rob and desired to have him coach the corners at Auburn is sufficient validation for me of Travaris's football knowledge, but I needed no validation of T-Rob the person. I knew it when we were teammates, and I could gather a locker room full of former brothers who would undoubtedly echo the very same sentiment.

Welcome home, T-Rob, and do not change. Usher in an emotion and mind-set of defensive football that mirrors the way you approach life, the way you played, the person you are. Your former teammates are proud of, and for, you. Your Auburn family is grateful for your decision to come home. Your Auburn defense can use your passion to play the game the way you did. We wait excitedly to see your influence on all you touch.

CHAPTER FIVE

Impact of Coaching on Lives

One of the greatest benefits of participation in athletics is learning how to be coached by someone other than a parent. Other than my father, coaches in my life were easily the most influential and impactful on my growth and development beyond the athletic fields. Not every coach was great; in fact, some were unequivocally atrocious. But even the bad apples provided a unique learning experience.

Receiving instruction from poor coaches prepared me for receiving instruction from poor teachers, poor employers, and poor leadership. I learned the tough lesson of respecting authority when doing so is incredibly difficult. Those are invaluable life teachings that can't be imparted in every forum.

Poor coaching also teaches kids about their parents. It's difficult to remain silent when you disagree with the instruction being given to you, or you are convinced that you could perform more effectively and efficiently in a different way. Parents have an innate intuition to jump in and save the day for their children. When that happens, the child may be relieved of poor coaching for the moment, but by not being forced to deal with the situation on his own, he suffers the loss of a life lesson opportunity. Problem solving skills, learning to adapt, morphing a bad situation into a more positive one—these are unique opportunities athletics provides. I've grown immensely from poor coaches I've suffered under.

But the good ones have had a lasting effect in every aspect of my life in more positive ways than I can count. I have always maintained that the values of discipline, teamwork, punctuality, sportsmanship, respect for authority, commonality, finishing were ingrained in me before I left elementary school. My parents, teachers, and peers undoubtedly played a role in honing these attributes, but it was the coaches who most emphatically entrenched these core tenets into my very fabric.

Yes, coaches taught me the basic fundamentals of form tackling, lining up to play a ground ball, and the art of free-throw shooting. They demanded full-speed simulation, total concentration, eye contact, and devoted attention. They provided consistent structure, an environment of teaching, an ear willing to listen. They offered life parallels and regularly connected the work and sacrifice put forth on the practice field or weight room to real-world scenarios of a father, a husband, a child of God. These men were molding individuals for much more than success in athletics. They saw far beyond a star-studded baseball career, SEC caliber football success, a life built around glory through sports. They could see over that cliff we all get to, when athletics no longer dominate our every thought and action, when our bodies can no longer withstand the demands of the sport, when our skills fade in comparison to those who surround us. They were implanting skills, attitudes, and strategies for life—for when rocky times came, when the waves came crashing in, when the summit seemed too steep to scale.

Success in athletics? Great! Success academically? Even better! Not walking out on your marriage, quitting on your employer, neglecting your children? The ultimate goal! I can see that now as the lessons taught during my entire athletic career rush forth on a daily basis. My coaches were planting roots for victory in life. The demands to push deeper when I wanted to stop? It was the lesson of perseverance, breaking down the mental barriers we erect of our own limitations. The lectures on the necessity of teamwork, cohesiveness, trustworthiness and belief in your teammate? It was the lesson of unselfishness and altruism; life is not all about me, and if I wanted to be prosperous in my endeavors and particularly my relationships, the price would be hard work at cultivating relationships with those I love.

My most influential coaches were indisputably my football coaches. Perhaps that's because it's the sport in which I most flourished. Perhaps that's because it's the sport requiring the most physical and mental challenges. Whatever the reason, I had coaches at all levels who held enormous sway over who I became and continue to become.

Tim Cole was an assistant football coach I "endured" for six football seasons, from ages six to eleven. He expected nothing less than perfection. He tapped into my potential athletically, but also drove me mentally to play with a purpose, play with smarts, play like a champion. I can still hear his deep, gruff voice prompting me to push, fight, exceed, go all out. That voice has never faded in my life; in fact, the echo has only grown louder. He had no children my age. No skin in the game, so to speak. He saw a group of kids to whom he could impart the game of football, yet instilled so much more. I owe a great deal to Tim Cole.

Hal Riddle was my high school football coach. He was the antithesis of Tim Cole in demeanor and mannerisms. In a sport filled with testosterone-driven machismo, in a fiery environment packed with smart-mouthed, know-it-all high school teenagers, Coach Riddle provided the perfect contrast. He was reserved, quiet, compassionate, yet stern. He was also discipline-heavy, demanded excellence on and off the field, and was doggedly determined to graduate better people rather than simply better players. He was a model husband, and father to a group of guys who desperately needed to see how that played out in the life of a mentor. He taught me the lessons of humility, perseverance, and priorities in life. He will always be a father figure to me, and will never be Hal—always Coach.

Bill Oliver was the reason I became an Auburn Tiger. He was known and respected throughout football for being a defensive innovator, a coordinator esteemed for origination and results. He stressed the mental aspect of football: outsmarting, outflanking, outmaneuvering the opposition. He also obsessed over the details. Watching film in our meeting rooms was like watching surgery with Dr. James Andrews. He was the master; we were but neophytes hoping to glean a fraction of wisdom from his critique. He was the only coach I ever had who could simultaneously see the noseguard's gap alignment, the linebacker's stance, and my eyes at safety, all at the snap of the ball! His biggest requirements were quick feet, eye recognition, and hand utilization. He didn't care if you were a speedster, had the "measurables," or were a Parade All-American. To him, speed and athleticism without fantastic football smarts just meant a player out of position that much faster. I learned more about football in the two years I spent with Coach Oliver than in the fifteen years of football without him combined. Coach Oliver taught me to never underestimate your potential, never underestimate your opponent, and to never underestimate the necessity of proper preparation.

Column published at AuburnSports.com March 28, 2014, discussing the departure of Coach Phillip Lolley from the Auburn program:

In Tommy Tuberville's inaugural address to the Auburn football team just after my sophomore season in 1998, he told us he would be hiring two strength and conditioning coaches who could "physically throw" every player out of the weight room. The first of those two men was Coach Phillip Lolley, hired as the conditioning coach, but who in reality served as a defensive analyst. The second was Strength and Conditioning Coach Kevin Yoxall. Both left indelible footprints on Auburn football and Auburn players for years to come.

Coach Lolley would become a mentor for me. When Coach Tuberville changed our defensive philosophy from a 3-4 to 4-3, suddenly I was positionless. I was coming off a Coaches Second Team All SEC year at strong safety, and eager to take over as the top strong safety in the league. Suddenly the strong safety position did not exist in our new defense. Coach Lolley was the coach to whom I would express frustration about my new role as a blocking dummy and zone defender as a "rover." He hated what we were doing. He did not agree with our defensive coordinator. He would go to bat for new ideas, challenge strange techniques, argue tactical elements that were unsound. He wanted us to be comfortable and confident in our play, and advocated on our behalf on the practice field, in the film room, in coaches' meetings, and in the locker room during halftime adjustments. It was almost as though he was hired to play devil's advocate to the defensive coordinator, to say the things we wished we could but knew better than to voice our opinions.

Don't get the mistaken impression he was a pushover for players, or not loyal to his coaching superiors. He was intense on the field. He expected you to work your tail off and demanded effort and discipline daily. He had a plethora of coaching knowledge and experience to share, and was a terrific teacher of defensive football. If you find one Auburn defensive back from the last decade and a half who tells you Coach Lolley wasn't a positive influence in life and on the football field, I would be left utterly speechless. He cared deeply for us. And in a dog-eat-dog environment, where both players and coaches are in constant flux, Coach Lolley worked hard to gain our trust and establish lasting relationships. Players who trust their coaches, believe in their philosophy, and have faith their coaches will stand behind them no matter what, will play inspired football, will be better teammates, and will win more games than they probably should (look no further than the 2013 Auburn team to prove this point).

I remember walking down to field level prior to the 2011 Auburn-LSU game in Baton Rouge. LSU was a monster and Auburn had no quarterback. Coach Lolley was leaning up against a fence by the benches prior to warmups, and I asked him about the match-up. He minced no words. "We're about to get slaughtered!" he said. "Why?" I asked. "Because Gene wants to sit back and play zone defense. My guys want to challenge the hell out of these wideouts all over this damn field…and Rob, we could do it! We should make a below average quarterback make difficult throws. But we're not! We're gonna sit back and play zone and they're about to have their way with us. Pisses me off!" LSU went on to win 45-10, throwing three TDs. He was loyal to the core. Obedient to the point of pain. He loved Auburn and wanted to see Auburn on top.

When he left the field for his liaison role with high school coaches, he thrived and Auburn benefited immensely. It was hard for a high school coach from the black belt to relate to Eddie Gran or Trooper Taylor, charismatic guys but lifelong college coaches. In Coach Lolley they saw the realism and understanding of a high school guy. They saw themselves. He could relate to where they were coming from. It's the reason Gus Malzahn is so well liked by the high school coaches. They're a fraternity, and Coach Lolley was not only one of them, he was one of the all-time greats. His teams were his proof.

Whenever someone you're close to walks away from Auburn, you feel as if a piece of you is leaving with him. I felt that way with Coach Bill Oliver, and to a lesser extent with Coach Tuberville. But I certainly feel it with Coach Lolley's departure. He has been a loyal Auburn advocate, a dynamic piece of the puzzle, a guy called upon to fill a number of roles, a constant in the midst of tremendous change, a friend to many. Auburn is losing a valuable component when Phillip Lolley walks out the door. I know he'll succeed wherever he goes. I hope Auburn is prepared to hire a prodigy, because the shoes he's asked to fill will be quite large.

Thank you, Coach, for your service to Auburn. You'll be greatly missed!

These are not the only positive influential coaches in my lifetime. I have coaches I'm still close to at this moment, decades since I last played under their direction. Coaches who still have the power of halting whatever I'm doing to stop, listen, respect their opinion and time. Though I appreciate their calling and have benefited mightily from their tutelage, I envy no coach's decision to work with young people. Why? Because these men will be judged more critically, perhaps more harshly, one day by our Creator. Their influence over these kids is extraordinary; it's powerful. They're on the front lines with today's youth, and their impact has enormous potential for good. Is it being used wisely? How did they use their platform? Did they set the right example?

If you are a coach, I hope you'll make it an effort—a priority—to be more concerned about you and your teams winning in *life*, as opposed to winning on the scoreboard. Don't major in the minors and minor in the majors with your teams. The average coach can impact over 25,000 kids in their careers.[1] Twenty-five thousand! That's not my number; it's from Dr. Howard Hendricks at Dallas Theological Seminary. That number is staggering when you really consider it. By virtue of your profession, of being a football coach, you are a coach of influence. What that says to me is this:if all you're doing is coaching football, you're not doing enough!

I am a more complete, accomplished individual in large part because of the coaches with whom I've been lucky enough to be associated. The good that came from my time with great coaches far exceeded the results of any bad my time I spent with the poor coaches. I advocate strongly for sports because of the constructive force great coaches have.

[1]Arnold, Lori. Christian Examiner Online. COIN ministry supports, equips coaches as they mentor players. January 2012.

Reggie Torbor arrived at Auburn as an undersized defensive end from Baton Rouge, LA, without immense fanfare in 1999, yet left Auburn as one of the university's all-time leaders in sacks. A terrific teammate and soft-hearted person off the field, Reggie was a guy who was serious and devoted to becoming a better player, excelling to the point of earning a job with the New York Giants as a fourth-round draft pick in 2004. At New York, Reggie played for and won Super Bowl XLII in 2008 against the New England Patriots, 17-14—reaching the pinnacle of football. Along the way, Reggie was impacted by many coaches who positively influenced him in countless ways. He is now the influencer of young men as head

football coach of Restoration Academy, a faith-based Christian school in Fairfield, AL. "I'm excited to be the head football coach at Restoration Academy because it will give me the opportunity to disciple and fellowship with young people," he said at his introductory press conference in 2014. "I benefited greatly from the influence of mentors growing up, and I hope to do the same for the next generation of students." Obviously, Reggie is well aware that the impact he can have will extend far beyond the football field, touching many aspects of daily life for years to come.

Biography

The defensive recipient of the Eddie Welch Attitude and Effort Award from the coaching staff in 2003, Reggie Torbor came into his own as a senior at Auburn University, establishing himself as one of the top pass rushers in the South … Named the team's Most Improved Defensive Lineman as a sophomore … Was also a Freshman All-Southeastern Conference choice … Blessed with outstanding speed, Reggie played in forty-six games for the Tigers, recording 120 tackles (69 solos) with 19.5 sacks for minus 141 yards, 32 stops for losses of 174 yards, 10 pass deflections, five forced fumbles, three fumble recoveries, 52 quarterback pressures and a blocked kick … His 18.5 sacks rank fourth in school history, topped only by Craig Olgetree (21, 1986-89), Tracy Rocker (21, 1985-88) and Gerald Robinson (24, 1982-85) … Member of the New York Giants (2004-2007) ending with a Super Bowl ring; the Miami Dolphins (2008-2009), and the Buffalo Bills (2010-2011). Reggie and his wife, Michelle, have two sons, Reggie Jr. and Cameron.

Impact of Coaching

By Reggie Torbor

I've heard it said, "The only thing you can do alone in this world is fail." However, you don't realize the impact someone is making on your life until years have passed. I have shown up to many football practices over the years, hoping only to get better at the game of football. I didn't realize that my coaches would give me something much greater.

When I retired from the NFL in 2011, I told myself that I was done with football. I had played the game since I was seven, and I'd had enough. I never dreamed that I would become a football coach. God had other plans for my life.

I accepted the head football coaching position at a small private school in Birmingham, AL. I began putting together schemes for offense and defense, researching what would work best for our team. I know football. I've been blessed with the opportunity to learn from some great football minds. My plan was to implement my schemes and lead my team to victory. I would soon realize how useless my schemes were.

Shortly after accepting the job, one of my players came to see me in my office. He began to share with me the difficulties of his home life, and that it was beginning to affect his school work. I tried to explain to him that, although it seemed tough at the moment, it would be worth it later in life, once he achieved all of his goals. He looked at me as if he had never heard those words before—as if no one had ever told him that he had the power to change his life. This made me think back to 1995, my freshman year at Robert E. Lee High School in Baton Rouge, LA.

I was in Kevin LeMoine's wood-shop class. Mr. LeMoine, who also happened to be my head football coach, was asking me about the plans I had for my life. As I began to tell him how I only wanted to graduate high school and, hopefully, get a job at the local mill, I could see the disappointment on his face. Coach LeMoine told me that I could become anything if I worked hard. He told me to set some goals, and that he would do all he could to help me achieve them. He believed in me.

Now, almost twenty years later, as I sat in my office talking to this young man, I realized that he wasn't in need of a football playbook. He needed me to believe in him.

I had spent so much time trying to figure out what game schemes would work best, I forgot to think about *why* they worked. The best teams that I have played on weren't always the most talented. We were great because we were disciplined, accountable, hardworking, determined, selfless young men. All the long hours in the hot sun were meant to build each of these characteristics in us. My coaches understood that if we were strong in these areas it wouldn't matter what scheme they chose; we would be successful. They weren't as focused on building a good football team as they were on building strong young men. This is now my role as coach: a leader of men.

During my first week of spring practice as a head coach, we had a string of terrible practices. One evening, as I pulled up in my driveway feeling frustrated, I could hear the voice of Gene Chizik, my defensive coordinator at Auburn University. "Never let your circumstances determine your character." After taking a whipping from LSU my senior year, Coach Chizik explained to us that, as men, we have to remember who we are at all times. There are people who count on us. He began to explain how his kids don't care about the score of the game. All they know is that "Daddy's home!" They want the Daddy who throws them in the air while they laugh, not the Daddy who sits on the sofa and mopes all weekend. As this flashback brought a smile to my face, I walked into my home and kissed my wife and two boys. As it turns out, my coaches taught me how to do more than just tackle.

Coach Jack Crowe has seemingly coached everywhere. After a forty-year coaching career with stops as an offensive coordinator at such college football powers as Auburn, Clemson, Arkansas, and Baylor, as well as nearly two decades of head coaching stints at Arkansas and Jacksonville State University, few people are as well versed in offensive football as Jack Crowe. Coach Crowe and I began broadcasting live, unedited commentary on Auburn football beginning in 2013, and have also launched an Auburn-centric weekly telecast called* Auburn Intel. *Coach Crowe is easily one of the smartest football minds I have ever been around, and it is easy to see why he has become a success. I could think of no one better to discuss the effect players have had on his life as a longtime coach.

Coaching Biography

A native of Birmingham, AL, Jack Crowe has coached nearly forty years at some of the top programs in the country. During his career, he has worked at Auburn, Baylor, Arkansas, Clemson, and Wyoming on the Division I-A level, and also has college coaching stints at North Alabama and Livingston (now West Alabama).

Crowe got his start in coaching without playing college football. He played football and baseball at West End High School in Birmingham, then went to Jefferson State Junior College, where he stuck with baseball.

He transferred to UAB and, after graduating with a degree in chemistry, became an assistant at West End High School. A year later, he became offensive coordinator at Oxford High School, where the Yellow Jackets posted a 21-1-1 record and two conference titles.[1]

Coach Crowe recorded over one hundred wins as a collegiate head coach, and was an integral reason several teams played and won championships with him on the sideline.

[1]www.jsugamecocksports.com

Finding The Qualities—Players Impacting Coaches

By Jack Crowe

We have all heard that coaches affect players' lives beyond their days of football. I know that coaches had a lifelong effect on my life. I sense that I have also had that effect on some whom I have coached. But players of extraordinary qualities can in turn have a great effect on the people who coach them. Coaches in general coach everybody the same. A few times in my forty-year career I have experienced a paradigm shift in my coaching, because the talents or the intellect of a player were beyond the scope of any previous coaching experience. It caused me to compare an individual to every quarterback I had coached after Randy Campbell to him.

At Auburn in 1982, Alabama had a ten-year upper hand. In my first spring I had been directed by Pat Dye to develop a championship-caliber QB by the end of spring practice. I started with four QBs; two were high school All-Americans. Randy Campbell was signed as a QB, but was moved to wide receiver before I got to Auburn and was sixth on the depth chart there. As spring practice developed I did not think I had the championship caliber player we needed. Coach Larry Blakeney recommended moving Randy to QB somewhere in the process. He was small and on the slow side, but after a few weeks I could see his amazing football intellect. He made the players around him better because he knew how to run the team and how to consistently make the right decisions. And he had the champions marker: the more intense the situation the better he was at making plays.

Still, Pat and I had to come to an agreement to hand him the future of the Auburn program, and, in effect, our jobs.

A player who had only marginal skills was not a unanimous pick. Pat asked me after the spring A-Day game if the QB who was number one most of the spring was my pick and I said, "No." By then, Randy had reshaped my thinking about the position. Pat saw signs, too, and after a considerable discussion he took the team out on the next Monday night in an undercover scrimmage to finalize the position with the team. Randy showed us all that he could step it up. It still wasn't unanimous. One senior football administrator told me privately that my decision would get us all fired. I believed that Randy could overcome his every athletic shortcoming with his ability to manage the game. To this day he stands alone. I made every game plan around his innate ability to keep us out of a bad play, while playing every percentage advantage I could find. His consistency made Auburn a champion.

Auburn under the leadership of Randy Campbell was 20-4. We beat Alabama (back-to-back), won the SEC, and Randy earned himself a Bowl MVP and the Alabama Sportswriters Player of the Year. He redefined the role of the position for me. After Randy, my future QBs were judged against his qualities, and the closer they got to his scale the more I gave them of the "Randy Campbell" version of my coaching experience.

Randy not only affected my coaching; he affected the future of the Auburn program, along with Pat Dye, who believed in me enough to allow me to go through that paradigm shift. We both were better for having looked deeper into the character of an exceptional young man—who loved the game, his team and his university—to find his unique qualities.

CHAPTER SIX

When Adversity Strikes

"Sudden change! Sudden change!" This was the term roared by our coaches on the football field after our offense turned the football over. Some turnovers were more costly than others, each its own new burden to bear; but all shared some similarities. They were never opportune, always putting the defense in a difficult scenario. They were never planned for, always coming at an unexpected moment in a game. Always momentum swinging, providing the opponent a chance to benefit from our miscue. Always chaotic, as the defense rushes back onto the playing surface in the middle of discussions about adjustments with coaches, conversations with teammates about strategy, consultation with trainers about nagging injuries. A "sudden change" shout signified adversity and was a call to arms. It was our job to come together, extinguish the fire, and limit the damage.

Momentum means so much in athletics. Its power and effect is palpable to the players and coaches in the moment, extending effortlessly to the casual sports fan watching a game far away on television. Coaches implement game plans specific to the start of each contest in an effort to capture the early momentum. Garnering momentum is a high priority, because both player and coach understand that overcoming a team that now has momentum on its side is an unattractive assignment. Teams become superior and individual players' abilities seem to becme heightened when momentum is working synergistically. "Sudden change!" was a signal of potential momentum shift. It had to be addressed. There could be consequences that would vary, depending on thour response.

None of us is immune to adversity. Whether the form is financial hardship, medical misfortune, community crises, societal barriers, relational disputes, spiritual crossroads, occupational obstacles, or an infinite list of potential pitfalls, the road to adversity is wide and always finds its way to our doorstep. Athletics provides the footing in not only learning to deal with this fact of life but also in turning the momentum in our favor.

The 1998 football season for Auburn University was mired in problems, most of them the self-inflicted variety. For me, adversity in athletics equates to my sophomore season at Auburn. An inordinate number of bad things occurred during Terry Bowden's final season at Auburn...so many that trying to isolate just one as an example is a challenge. However, there is something that occurred during this campaign that was incredibly inexplicable. We managed to accomplish a feat that has to be some sick record in the bowels of NCAA worsts. For three consecutive weeks—first against LSU, then against Tennessee, then against Mississippi State—by the time we hit the field as a defensive unit, the opponent had already scored a touchdown. That's quasi-impossible.

LSU intercepts the first pass of the game and returns it for a touchdown. The next week against Tennessee, our offense drives the length of the football field inside the Tennessee ten yard line, only to watch a Tennessee defensive tackle intercept a wild pass and return over ninety yards for the opening score. At Mississippi State the comedy of errors reached its zenith. MSU was penalized fifteen yards before the game even began for unsportsmanlike conduct during warmups. They kicked off to us from their twenty yard line. On the kickoff we returned the ball safely. However, MSU was offsides. Coach Bowden elected for MSU to re-kick from the fifteen, all but assuring us excellent field position to start this road game. On the second kick, our returner fumbled the ball and an MSU defender scooped it up. As our second returner attempted to tackle the ball carrier, the MSU player pitched the ball to a teammate, who then strolled in to the end zone untouched for an MSU touchdown! They kicked off from their fifteen yard line and scored a touchdown on the play! I threw up in my mouth as I ran onto the field: for the third consecutive week, a touchdown before playing a down of football. Coach Bowden resigned/quit/was fired the next week. Adversity! That team had it, and it crushed us. But it also transformed us and ushered in a new mind-set far removed from the misery that unchecked adversity and a tidal wave of negative momentum had saturated us with.

Coach Tommy Tuberville piloted a new psyche into our program. Yes, from harder work than we had known; yes, from a new accountability with which we were unaccustomed. But, predominantly, our new direction stemmed from the relationships we developed with one another, the understanding we drew from each other, the appreciation we gathered from the collective as we prayed together in our team prayer meetings. The misery of failure stoked a spiritual renewing. The spiritual renewing generated a unit willing to lie down and die for one another. We were not talented enough to warrant a Western Division Championship in 2000, Coach Tuberville's second season. But when you've lived through the adversity of 1998, it takes paradigm shift to undergo a metamorphosis. We received that through the unifying spirit prayer meetings provided. The momentum turned and adversity was the catalyst.

Growth is often the product of struggle. Things that come easily rarely make us better people. In life, it is not a matter of *if* adversity will strike; it is a matter of *when*. It doesn't have to break us. It doesn't have to derail us from our goals. It doesn't have to end marriages, tear apart families, end employment, disintegrate our spirit. Use the adversity in your life to make you better. It's the hard lessons we most remember. As the old proverb goes, "Good timber does not grow with ease; the stronger the wind, the stronger trees."

Phillip Lutzenkirchen was a standout tight end/H-back for Auburn University from 2009–2012. He holds the Auburn record for most touchdowns by a tight end, and was known for several game-winning touchdowns throughout his career. Phillip was killed in the summer of 2014, a passenger in a single-car accident. Due to the circumstances surrounding the accident, in which the driver and Phillip were both intoxicated, Phillip's father Mike Lutzenkirchen now travels extensively speaking to groups about the dangers of drunk driving and the importance of the decisions we make. If you are not affiliated with Auburn University, the level of despair and grief the death of Phillip Lutzenkirchen had on the Auburn family cannot be adequately described in written word. Below is my futile attempt to express the grief the Auburn faithful felt.

The Fragility of Life: The Inexplicable Death of Phillip Lutzenkirchen

Published July 2, 2014 at AuburnUndercover.com

"My brother is invincible..." was the first Twitter message I saw after learning of the news of the tragic death of Phillip Lutzenkirchen. It was written by his sister, Abby, who more so than any of us suffered untold anguish and agony at the loss of her big brother. Her hero, her confidant, her relationship with a sibling we all have adored for a few short years, yet whom she has admired for a lifetime, was gone. The life of an Auburn great, the epitome of an Auburn man, taken from us in an instant. We mourn. The Lutzenkirchen family is shattered.

The death of "Lutz" is a reminder of the fragility of life. It's a reminder of the urgency of eternity. It's a reminder of tomorrow being promised to no one. It's a reminder that the young men and women who represent our universities with stunning athletic aptitude are indeed human beings. They are capable of hurt, capable of gaffes, and heartbreakingly capable of untimely death.

I think that often we look at these young people as superhuman. Our first encounter with them is via a high school highlight tape, in which they appear to be Greek gods, utterly dominating competitors who are vastly inferior in talent. We know it's not reality, but we envision that same dominance in orange and blue jerseys because we have been sold on their stardom.

We see the competition on game day, the rival team bus into our domain, onto our campus, into our stadium and we greet them with taunts, with jeers, with profanity, with the insinuation of impending physical harm. Far from a friendly jaunt to a member institution, game days are better portrayed in ancient Roman coliseums, where the participants are expendable for the entertainment of the crowd.

While players enter these unfriendly environments fully aware they are protected from the off-the-field elements, the feeding-frenzied atmosphere, the rabid nature of the venom hurled from regular, educated, everyday football fans is shocking. It's part spectacular tradition and part asinine obliviousness that so much hope is resting on young men from home, and so much hate is hurled at the young men visiting.

When we hear the news of someone as revered and respected, adored and adulated as Phillip Lutzenkirchen yielding to the limits of humanity, his life ending at a dark intersection in western Georgia in a tragic car accident, suddenly the immortal becomes human. It's dreadful for all us to accept such a promising figure, the model humanitarian, the picture of health, prominence and renown taken from this earth way too soon. How do we deal with that? What do we learn from that?

I think Phillip's life held all the answers to these difficult questions. He attacked life with the same determination and positive attitude as he did the game of football. How do we deal with tragedy? We deal with it one day at a time. We give thanks for each day and live it as though it's the last. We see the positive influence in the life of others that we hope to see in those who surround us. We choose to have fun, to not take life so seriously, and to be gracious and loving toward opposing points of view or divergent cultural norms. We learn that he who provides for this life but fails to take care of eternity may be wise for a brief moment, but he's a fool forever. We learn to nurture relationships with our family members because they're family, they're blood. We learn to overcome adversity, just as Phillip had to at the end of his football career.

In a mere twenty-three years, the manner in which Lutz lived personified the Auburn spirit. He literally could have been the face, the calling card, for what it meant to be an Auburn man.

I have read numerous comments about Phillip smiling down on us from heaven, watching Auburn games, God needing him there, etc. The truth of the matter is this: Phillip Lutzenkirchen on the whole did not die; Lutz merely went to be with God. As a Christian, Lutz received life everlasting at the moment he accepted Jesus Christ as his Lord. Because of that, rest assured Lutz is alive. His spirit is with the Lord, and he is experiencing the joy and satisfaction he brought to so many in an incalculable measure. I don't want to speak for him, but I believe he would tell us the same.

We mourn Lutz. We grieve with the Lutzenkirchen family. We cry together as an Auburn family united behind a favorite son. We'll never forget Phillip Lutzenkirchen and the impact he made on us all.

I think we all strive to leave things better than the way we found them. Few of us can say we made that type of impact on the university we love. Phillip Lutzenkirchen made Auburn University a better place, and for that we are forever grateful.

CHAPTER SEVEN

Perseverance

In football it was gassers. In baseball it was foul poles. In basketball it was suicides. They were all dreadful conditioning drills in the three sports I played. They always came at the conclusion of practice, when strength and energy were things of the past, and fatigue and thirst were neon images brightly emblazoned upon my psyche. Humid summer conditions in the Deep South, combined with an overzealous importance placed upon athletics in general—football in particular—created miserable conditions under which to train. Yes, the value of athletics was undeniable, but the obsession, the adoption, the infiltration of athletics into our culture created an environment of over-exaggerated significance the adults placed upon the young athletes. Yet even as a young kid, I pushed myself to the extreme because that's what my coaches demanded. "If it doesn't kill you it'll make you stronger—and nobody's died yet!" was heard nearly every day. There was nothing enjoyable about conditioning in any sport, until you outlasted your opponent all the way to victory. Then you appreciated the sacrifice. Learning to persevere was not an easy lesson, but certainly one that was worthwhile.

Each of us in life will have valleys through which we must persevere. None of us is immune or shielded from infirmities that will strike. Athletes have been conditioned to fight through the pain, to dig deeper than what your mind allows, knowing the pain is temporary but the reward will be sweet justice. Innumerable examples of athletes overcoming injuries, mistakes, off the field turmoil, mental blocks, and even handicaps, inspire and stir emotion in us all. But two stories stand out to me that prove what mental toughness and perseverance instill in the athlete carries far beyond the playing surface.

Laura Hillenbrand's book *Unbroken* chronicles the life of Louis Zamperini, a chilling yet inspirational story of perseverance through the horrors of survival in Japanese prisoner of war camps during WWII. Of all the torture, physical, mental and spiritual, this man endured at the hands of Japanese enemy soldiers, it was Zamperini's battle against isolation, drifting at sea for forty-seven days on a raft fighting Mother Nature, that most astounded me. The will to live; the desire to keep his mind sharp; the ingenuity to find food given the opportunity; the strength to overcome hunger, weakness, dehydration, hypothermia—is so far removed from the inner resolve in most of us, it's inconceivable.

Sharks attempting to jump into his raft he beat off with an oar. Birds that landed on his raft, or on his body, he plucked with his bare hands. Rain that fell sporadically he captured and hoarded as drinking water. Forty-seven days at sea with nothing but two other frightened soldiers. I can't imagine the awfulness. I'm certain Louis Zamperini had several life experiences to that point which must have provided the impetus and drive to cheat death, to battle for life, to never give up. At the DNA level he was somehow made to survive.

But his story stemmed first and foremost from his athletic background as an Olympic miler. His grit, in large part, was a consequence of his athletic training and the perseverance that running at the highest level in the world imparted. His tale surely would not have ended as well without his athletic background bleeding over into his inner being and providing the doggedness to survive. His story cries *perseverance* like none other's I've ever heard nor seen.

Until recently, the news of another former athlete reverting back to his instinctive mode of perseverance to save his life is that of former NFL running back Rob Konrad's twenty-seven-mile swim to the Florida coast after falling off his fishing boat at sea. Konrad, who played for the Miami Dolphins from 1999 to 2004, roughly my age and sharing my background in athletics, found himself in the unenviably deadly position of being stranded at sea without the aid of a raft or life preserver.

While fishing alone and with his boat set on autopilot, a wave slamming against his thirty-one-foot boat sent Konrad overboard, his boat continuing east without him. It was 12:30 in the afternoon when Rob entered the water; the shore was nowhere in sight. He began swimming in the direction of shore, interchanging swimming strokes to prevent fatigue and concentrating on his young daughters for motivation to live. He endured stings of all kinds, an encircling shark, and the treachery of swimming nearly sixteen hours to shore. A Coast Guard helicopter and private fishing boats looked for him but did not spot him.

Upon hitting the beach, exhausted, dehydrated, surely hypothermic, indisputably frail, and unable to even walk, he was forced to crawl out of the water. His boat was found near the Grand Bahama Island on Deadman's Reef. Here again was a story of incredible perseverance by a former athlete using his mental fortitude to power his physical abilities.

With God's grace and under his watchful eye, hopefully none of us will be required to persevere to the extent of these two brave ex-athletes. Their stories are legendary; their feats improbable and certainly heroic. Each of us, however, can rest assured life will unfurl challenges before us that will test our perseverance. It takes a very special individual to withstand the mental anguish, the spiritual and emotional devastation, and the physical clout to not succumb to the conditions the two above encountered. But it also takes remarkable dedication and commitment to persevere in a marriage that has gone wayward, a job that requires daily sacrifices, and a child who is reliant on you to provide each and every meal he or she eats.

Life promises to present steep summits to scale, not all of equal height, with some seemingly insurmountable, when perseverance is called into action. Athletes certainly do not succeed in beating back all of life's problems; we have not cornered the market on perseverance supremacy in all things. But athletes certainly have the benefit of ingrained characteristics of steadfastness deep within their being. We have struggled and sacrificed on playing surfaces, weight rooms, under terrible conditions, with nagging injuries robbing us of our best efforts. We have overcome environments that would torment and haunt less mentally tough peers for years to come. We have been on the verge of defeat, only to find a way to battle back to victory. We have seen coaches and the relationships we've built instantaneously evaporate as coaches are fired and replaced with new coaches, with new plans, new personalities, and new schemes. We have entered contests no one believed we could win, and defied the odds. We have been pushed beyond limits we erected in our own minds—limits we were certain could not be moved, only to see them obliterated.

Participation in sports doesn't make you perfect, far from it. In fact, it magnifies your weaknesses for others to easily identify.

But athletics does force you into difficult circumstances and demands your greatest effort to emerge triumphant. Athletics teaches perseverance in large quantities, and Louis Zamperini and Rob Konrad prove that it stretches far beyond the playing surface, long after the glory days are gone.

Ben Leard and I share a special connection. We have lost count of the number of times well intentioned Auburn football fans have mistaken one of us for the other. I would receive notes and letters of well wishes in the weekly Tiger Walk trek to the stadium that were meant for Ben. He may have someone call him Rob at the airport. There have been more than a few times I have finished conversations with people never telling them I am not Ben. It's an ongoing joke with us. What was not a laughing matter was Ben's harsh entry into the starting quarterback position at Auburn University as a sophomore in

1998. Playing behind a makeshift offensive line riddled with injuries and inexperience, and the reality of a running game threat that was nonexistent, Ben struggled to find success early in his career, as any young quarterback without an arsenal of weapons would. He endured finger pointing and the casting of stones, not only from disapproving fans but from his very own teammates. He was benched by one coaching staff, and failed to win the starting quarterback battle to begin the next season with a new staff in place. He did not quit, sulk or lose confidence in his ability to contribute. He entered during the second half of the first game of the 1999 season—called upon to spark an anemic offense and tossed the game winning touchdown pass, never looking back and solidifying his place in the Auburn record books from that point on. He was our undisputed leader on the field, garnering All-Conference honors by the time we were seniors. But it was the way he handled his rocky collegiate start that left an indelible impression upon me, and that I've never forgotten. I've always known Ben Leard would be a success, regardless of the avenue of life he was forced to traverse, because I witnessed firsthand the manner in which he overcame criticism and disbelief on the part of those who surrounded him, thanks to a dogged resoluteness to not only prove he belonged, but to prove excellence.

Stubborn, Hard-headed, and Driven

By Ben Leard

As athletes, the terms resilience, perseverance, and dedication are used frequently. I am also of the opinion that a few others should be added to the mix: stubborn, hard-headed, and driven carry a very similar connotation. Not only does this ring true as an athlete prepares for competition, it also is the case during his respective event. You can also translate this to all levels of corporate America, as well as being a parent and spouse.

Now, I mean this in the most positive of ways. Time and time again we are knocked down by injury, competitors, adversity, etc. But we contine to push ourselves to get back up and go at it again. The politically correct term is, and would be referred to by ESPN as, "resilient" or "dedicated." Well, simply replace that with stubborn and you can pretty much reach the same description of an individual's gumption. Everyone who has accomplished a measure of success carries these traits. They have overcome some type of relative adversity with flying colors. Athletes must be stubborn and hard-headed. But in a coachable way, of course. You are pushed beyond all limits as you prepare or condition. You are told more than one time that "you can't do that" or "that won't work." But, for some intrinsic reason, we don't quit because it's not in our nature. We hold the line and continue to push forward, never retreating even in the most dire of situations. It is how we've been trained; it's how we are wired.

Again, translate that into being a parent, a soldier, an employee, a boss. It all comes back to the same common denominator. In the boardroom you will be beaten. Do you pack up and never return? Absolutely *not*! You hit harder the next time. You prepare harder. You study more. You combat all possible hypotheticals. So, when the next opportunity arises, you own it and can stand tall in victory. As a parent, if times get tough, what do you do? Stay in bed. Run away. Quit. No you don't. You can't, because you have people relying solely on you. Being persistent in that drive to provide is and should be unwavering. Or is that being stubborn and not letting anything keep you down? Either way you want to categorize it is fine, because the same result should be yours at the end of that effort.

Taking it one step farther, this is where you'll find your most stubborn and hard-headed individuals, who are your *leaders*. I'm a firm believer that you can't make or manufacture a leader. Either you have it or you don't. It's just a matter of tapping into that piece of your brain and heart to determine if you have what it takes to stand in front and lead, or should you be a faithful follower and provide your talents in support. Leaders possess the ability to translate their desires in a motivational but informative manner. It's a gift that you are born with, and it is simply sharpened by mentors or other leaders. As a leader you have to continuously subject yourself to scrutiny and criticism. Therefore, you take resiliency and stubbornness to the next level. You have to, or you will fail. A successful leader will address his troops, team, employees or family, and then turn his back to them. Why? Because he or she is standing on the front lines, and will be the first to take on the adversity or adversary, as the case may be. You don't watch your people battle. You fight alongside or in front of them.

"It is not the critic who counts. The credit belongs to the man who is actually in the arena ... who at the best knows the triumphs of high achievements, and who at the worst, if he fails, at least fails while daring greatly, so that his place will never be with those cold and timid souls who know neither victory nor defeat"—*Theodore Roosevelt.* One of the true gifts of a good leader is to understand motivation as well. Not everyone will allow a fire and brimstone speech to resonate. Some need a simple "atta boy" every once in a while. Others need to be managed to a microscopic degree, while others don't. Identifying them is very difficult, and remembering it is a talent within itself. Push hard but know when to pump the brakes. High expectations are a good thing, but you must be prepared to address the fact that you may not reach that bar. Stay the course and remain driven, stubborn, and hard-headed. Failure is imminent. We are all going to lose at some point. The question is, What are you going to do as a result of that loss? Quit or get better? "A leader is one who knows the way, goes the way, and shows the way"—*John C. Maxwell.* Whether you are male/female, black/white, athlete/business person, soldier/employee ... it does not matter. All who achieve a measure of success in our field of expertise are stubborn, hard-headed and driven. You can choose to use the politically correct terms of resiliency or perseverance if you want. But I will stick with what I as, a father, businessman, and former athlete, understand. The blunt straightforward terminology that has proven itself to me for many years, and will continue to do so for many more. Regardless of the hurdles, stay in it and never quit. The harvest at the end of the growing season is beyond reward and will pay residual benefits to you and those around you a hundredfold.

CHAPTER EIGHT

Dealing with Diversity: Athletics and Race Relations

Ignorance is the harbinger of fear. For many, the less we know about something or someone the more anxiety it produces when we are surrounded by it. For those growing up in the deep south, race relations has always been contentious. It stems predominately from a poor understanding of cultural divides; of the struggles for freedoms and acceptance some take for granted; of the divergence in how we worship, what we wear, how we speak, what we listen to, how we relate to others. Differences bring about contempt when an ingrained societal belief system dominates the spirit and permeates a culture. All races of people tend to flock toward their own because we find comfort in similarities. The homogenous make-up of communities, churches, teams, schools, and businesses is understandable, considering the stereotypes and thought patterns ingrained in our cultures. The sad reality is that the diversity we fear and which separates us prevents us from enriching one another, learning from each other, working together for common purposes, seeking and enjoying unity.

Sport is light years ahead of society with regard to race relations. I'm appreciative for my experiences in athletics that have enabled me to build trust, friendships, respect, and acceptance among teammates who look very different than I do. More than teammates, these young men are brothers to me, guys for whom I would have then, and to this day would now, lay down my life. Society, politics, cultural reservations, "race-baiters" all seek to erect barriers, spew hatred, scream loudly about what divides us in an effort to maintain influence, power, and payouts. The commonality we share, the passions we hold dear, the way of life we strive to achieve do not make for good press points, TV shows, or story lines. Division, finger-pointing, fear mongering—all stemming from unfamiliarity, greed, the desire to retain power—drives a wedge between the worlds we live in. It's a shame.

As a peewee football player in the northeastern Birmingham suburb of Center Point, I was introduced to boys who did not live as I did. Some had no fathers. Some had no beds. Even school attendance was a spotty obligation. Some had no authority figure in their lives beyond a football coach across town. Without that football coach, some would have eaten many fewer meals and had little to no instruction and discipline in early life. We didn't care as players. Marquis could run like a deer, was quick off the ball, was hilarious to be around. Desmond was tough, could make an open field tackle against anyone, was a blast to hang out with. We saw the living conditions, the skin color, the wardrobe, the slang, and saw a person, a teammate, a friend. We loved those guys. We didn't feel sorry for them, take it easy on them, try to appease them, make concessions because of them. They were part of our team; therefore, they were part of us. They were family. We held each other accountable, pushed each other to improve, and ultimately enjoyed many years of dominance in youth football across the state and south.

Several high school teammates in football, basketball, and baseball were black. Never one time did we have an issue with race. And how could that be? We hit each other daily. We yelled at each other. We trash talked each other. We were put in uncomfortable situations when we were fatigued. We competed against each other in an environment full of masculinity and testosterone, seemingly conducive to common bouts of emotional explosion. Yet what I found was that, instead of these things dividing us, they were unifying. We had a goal, a mission, a creed, an understanding, a reliance, a belief, a respect in the teammate beside you, color be damned. We loved and cared for each other because we shared mutual goals. We wanted to be champions. Wanted to taste success. Athletics united us in ways nothing else in society could.

When I became an Auburn Tiger, I was the only scholarship white defender on the football team who traveled and played. In a defensive meeting room I was the lone white guy. In the defensive backfield I was the lone white guy. My teammates could have made that very difficult for me if they wanted to. They could have shunned me, could have not embraced me for my obvious lack of melanin. They could have treated me as a foreigner, a castaway, and made life miserable for me. I was outnumbered and surrounded by others unlike me. Society would say I'd never make it. Athletics would beg to differ.

Not only did my teammates go far beyond token acceptance and obligatory conversation and relationships, they took me under their wing. They protected me, fought for me, taught me the defense, refined my technique. They were grooming me for success on Saturday because they needed to be able to count on me. They knew that their success, our team success, hinged on me being successful as well. They joked with me, teaching me black fraternity signs and prodding me to "throw them up" after a good play on the field. They joked with me about heading down to Tuskegee after games to hang out with the black ladies. I joked with them by learning the lyrics to popular rap songs, busting out with one on occasion. I joked with them by "revealing" that my speed was passed down from my black grandmother. In fact, in crucial moments of big games, I would promise that if we get a three and out on this drive I'm going to Tuskegee tonight! We would run onto the field with guys yelling, "Pate going to 'Skegee!" We got several of those three and outs. I never lived up to the promise (I was engaged or married during my entire Auburn tenure). We had no bitterness toward each other. We didn't allow society to separate us with a false narrative. We didn't view ourselves as superior in athleticism, intellect, or privilege. We were just friends, brothers, teammates, equals, family. We hurt for each other, prayed for each other, laughed together, battled together. Athletics unified us just as athletics has for every team I've participated with since age five. It's one of the more unheralded aspects of sport. It has the power to bridge a social gulf like little else. It can force the most hardened heart to work with a dissimilar person towards a goal. It has been the impetus for relationships and experiences in my life that I otherwise would likely have never experienced. I believe I am a more well-rounded, enriched, empathetic person because of the people athletics has placed around me. If more people in our country had the same experience I did regarding race through athletics, the Jesse Jacksons and Al Sharptons would no longer have the same influence. The white supremacist movement or lurid racism would yield few followers. Those forces seek to divide us based on the differences we have inherited. Athletics does the exact opposite. It brings together people from worlds apart and teaches them to coalesce to obtain success. Politics can't do that. Society isn't doing that. Religion doesn't do that. Athletics does. You want your children to build a healthy, respectful, thoughtful outlook towards diversity? Sign them up to play on athletic teams with dissimilar races. You and your child will benefit immensely, as will society.

Stanford Simmons was the top-rated high school safety in the state of Alabama our senior season, and one of the most highly coveted recruits in the nation. He was a highly decorated defensive back from Clay County High School, notching Parade All-American and Super All-State status for his outstanding play. He and I were roommates and the starting safeties for team Alabama in the Alabama-Mississippi All Star Game following our senior year in high school. I had always played with black teammates in various sports growing up, but Stanford was my first black roommate. We are as similar and dissimilar as possible, at the same time. We went through the same recruitment, played the same position, chose the same university, but looked different (buzz cut versus corn rows), spoke differently, and were on opposite ends of the academic spectrum. He is a quality person, a good friend, a brother I love.

A Perspective from the Black Athlete

By Stanford Simmons

Being a black man in an environment where I had to be around, and socialize and develop relationships with, people of other cultures and other races was a challenge. As black athletes in sports, we sometimes put ourselves in situations that set us up for failure by attempting to use our talents alone to make up for the other aspects of the game. As the level of competition rises from high school to college, the commitment to being more than just a great athlete has to be high. Everyone is a great athlete at Auburn University, and I think some of the black athletes felt their athleticism alone would be enough to out-compete non-blacks for starting positions. This was not the case.

For instance, take a person with less talent who plays the game in a way that looks a little different, but it is obvious he is not as gifted with talent for the sport. He makes up for it by learning the finer points of the game, the details, the fundamentals, so that he depends less on talent to level the playing field. I saw in many cases more talented black players who played less than white teammates simply because the white guy knew the game better. I have played with guys who were less talented than me, but who made more plays than I did due to being in the right place at the right time.

From strictly a sports point of view, playing alongside a different race and the cultural differences that come with that, you learn a lot from other people. They think differently and go about things in a different way. People tend to grow and depend on each other when they are fighting for a common cause. Just like a baby is born without an understanding of trust or love or friendship, you can grow to learn and trust and appreciate and believe in the guy who is of a different race.

We may see things a bit differently, but we both need each other to reach the goals we have both set. "We" and "team" become greater than the individual player and just "my individual circumstance." You sweat, bleed, shed tears, and enjoy moments together, and the common ground allows that person to become your brother.

When you think you can't go any further, and you can't make it any longer, that person comes around to lift you up, and to tell you that you *can* do it. He's pushing you; and, although it's painful in the moment, it's a great feeling realizing you are not fighting that battle alone. That person who does not look like you, was not raised like you, is not your race, still shows you his love while you are going through pain. He willingly comes back for you, he walks beside you, he throws his arm around you while he is going through the same pain. He refuses to leave his teammate, brother, friend, a loved one behind.

When you endure that together, it throws racism out of the game and makes the world a slightly better place. The world would be a better place if people of any color were so considerate of others during times of struggle as teammates are. We have to live life together, and in football we were all as one. We had to grow to learn and appreciate each other. As with most things, we did not always agree, but we learned to sit down and work out issues by meeting each other half way. Team work is what wins, so let's work together and make this world a place where we all can be champions. Jesus Christ is the example. We just have to follow his lead.

Finally, I would like to give thanks to a person who is special to me—a friend, roommate, teammate, and brother: Rob Pate. Thank you, and War Damn Eagle!

CHAPTER NINE

Dealing with Great Expectations

Great accomplishment breeds pronounced expectations. Winning on the field, succeeding in the classroom, achieving in the workplace, overcoming the odds to prevail—all equate to an anticipation of continued attainment. Expectations are a part of life; many are so routine we give them no thought until they fail us. A repetitive beating heart, the timely sunrise, drawing clean drinking water from the faucet, the discomfort of a needle prick, the tax bill arriving in the mailbox. We presume these events without much fanfare because they are predictable. That predictably dampens our appreciation, diminishes our surprise when they occur. Sometimes this is beneficial, yet it can rob us of joy.

As an optometrist, I deal with unrealistic expectations every day. Superb vision is a gift often taken for granted by those blessed with it. It is not until seemingly everlasting crisp acuity fades to blur that the joy of sharp vision is truly appreciated and desperately desired. Ask anyone over the age of forty about the deleterious effects of age on vision and you'll receive a snicker and snide comment or two.

Optometry is a unique profession as it relates to how we are judged by our patients. We could detect the onset of diabetes or a brain tumor years before systemic discovery, yet be considered failures because of an inability to live up to the visual hopes of our patients. None are more demanding and unreasonable than multifocal contact lens wearers. These are people who wear a miniscule device, wettable enough to stay lubricated on the eye, permeable enough to allow oxygen to penetrate the lens, with optics working to correct multiple distances at the same time across a small space.

It's a challenge. There is an adaptation that must occur, and there must be a willingness to accept imperfection. Just like any defense in sports, there is always a weakness. The wearers who have reasonable expectations enjoy the positive aspects of the lens and relish wearing them. The wearers who perceive only the negatives, the limitations of the design and the device's inability to solve every nuanced focal length, never adjust and are dispirited. The difference between the two patient types is perception and expectations.

Teams fall prey to lofty expectations all the time in athletics. Aspirations, goals, ambitions—these are necessary and healthy for every team and every individual within that unit. It is what motivates and drives you to not simply finish a practice, but, rather, to master a skill, improve a technique, hone team chemistry every time out on the practice field. Teams and individuals operating without the desire to improve and develop on a daily basis set themselves up for failure. It is vitally important to grasp the significance of unity with regard to objectives, and for everyone to pull in the same direction working to make them come to fruition.

Sometimes, however, irrational expectations are placed upon teams, whether they arise from a fan base, the media, the coaching staff, or even from the players themselves. Unrealistic expectations, when placed upon a team and subsequently not met, can be the forerunner of discord and conflict. For instance, consider a team returning ten starters off a record-setting offense including the quarterback. On the surface, the expectation is that the previous record will be shattered; another year in the system with a returning quarterback equals elevated success for the new group. We expect, at the very least, to match last season's output, but deep down we are thinking that merely equaling last year's numbers would be a shame considering who is returning.

The expectations are set without regard to schedules, continuity, adjustments and/or schemes created to slow down our attack, or even personal issues arising in the lives of those who return that may differ from last year. Because of the elevated expectation, when not fulfilled we are less joyful. Winning becomes less fun because it is failing to meet our expectations of exactly what winning should look like. The team feels the negativity cast over their efforts and begins to press, and the result can be an unnecessary self-inflicted downward spiral due solely to an attempt to meet their own haughty expectations, even if a successful season's victory totals match—but just don't exceed—the previous year's I am not against setting goals, or expectations. I expect my government to keep my family safe with clean drinking water, a capable infrastructure, and a strong national defense. I expect my employees to show up on time and to treat patients with compassion. I expect my children to show respect, be honest, give their best efforts. I expect my wife and myself to honor our marriage vows. I expect the Auburn Tigers to play passionate football every time they take the field. The difference between expectations that are healthy and expectations that are toxic is their reasonability. And whether they are within reason is in the eye of the beholder. Athletics has helped to arm me with the capability of discerning reasonable expectations in life situations.

Marriages fail because of unmet expectations. Businesses go bankrupt because customer expectations are not reached. Individuals choose suicide over life because lofty expectations are never attained. Expectations are inescapable, a product of life. Healthy, pragmatic prospects stemming from reverential realism allow for contentment.

In truth, dealing with expectations is simply a part of life. Athletes, at any level but in particular those having competed at a high level in their sport, have the distinct advantage of dealing squarely with expectations and prospects of all kinds. They understand what it means to have a teammate expect them to deliver on their given assignment. They recognize the impact the weakest link has on the entire enterprise. They are cognizant of what will be required of them physically and mentally to secure and maintain a meaningful role on their team. They know what it means to battle through adverse circumstances, when the pressure is so thick it could be hacked away at with an axe, and the outcome hinges on executing with precision. They feel and hear the weight of exceedingly high expectations from fans and friends and family on a daily basis, a constant reminder of the uphill climb toward success.

Athletes have failed to meet expectations on multiple occasions, and in many ways. We learn from it, grow from it, and move on. But athletes have also looked great expectations squarely in the eye and have risen to the occasion to satisfy them. Expectations, whether great or miniscule, can be positioned in a way to motivate athletes in a way that the non-athlete can scarcely grasp. Sports have forced us to deal with expectations, preparing us for life's daunting tasks.

A three-year starter at middle linebacker for Auburn University from 2010-2013, Jake Holland had a collegiate career that was a roller coaster ride, to say the least. As a true freshman. Jake contributed on a 14-0 National Championship team, only to see things move south in a hurry. In Jake's junior year, Auburn endured a horrific 3-8 season, going winless in conference play. Coach Gene Chizik's firing ushered in Coach Gus Malzahn and his new staff for Jake's senior season. In the greatest turnaround in the history of college football, the 2013 Auburn squad returned to the National Title game, coming a mere thirteen seconds short of two titles in four years.

Jake's personal journey was just as up and down. His fourth and final year brought about a third defensive coordinator. He seldom made it through a season without injuries that undoubtedly lessened the caliber player he could have been. He constantly endured his own fan base's belittlement and vitriol, despite earning the starting linebacker role for three different head men. I can think of no former Auburn player better suited to speak on the topic of overcoming adversity.

Biography

Attended Pelham High School in Pelham, AL. No. 8-rated inside linebacker and the No. 10 player in Alabama by Rivals.com ... No. 8-rated middle linebacker by ESPN.com/Scouts Inc. ... No. 12-rated middle linebacker by Scout.com ... ranked as the No. 12 player in Alabama by SuperPrep ... named to the All-Southeast Region team by PrepStar ... ranked twentieth among middle linebackers by Tom Lemming on Maxpreps.com ... selected to the 2009 6A All-State Team by the Alabama Sports Writers Association as a senior ... 2010 Under Armour All-American game ... No. 10 on the Birmingham News' list of the Alabama Super Seniors ... ranked twelfth on the Mobile Press Register's 2009 Elite 18 ... No. 109 on the Mobile Press Register's Super Southeast 120 ... Orlando Sentinel 2009 All-Southern football team ... finished his high school career with 351 tackles ... totaled 153 tackles, 16 tackles for loss, a sack, four pass breakups, four forced fumbles, three interceptions and three fumble recoveries as a senior ... 129 tackles (74 solo) as a junior to go along with two sacks, eight quarterback hurries, one interception, one fumble recovery and five forced fumbles. A three-year starter at linebacker at Auburn under three different defensive coordinators. National champion and two-time SEC champion.

Overcoming Adversity

By Jake Holland

Throughout my athletic career, I've had to face adversity many times. Like many kids growing up in the south, I fell in love with sports, specifically football. I began my football journey at the age of six. I was given the opportunity to play in high school, college, and even a tryout in the NFL. I know I have been blessed in so many ways, but while there were highs, there were also lows.

Growing up, playing football was always an escape for me. It allowed me to express myself in ways nothing else could. I specifically enjoyed the mental aspect of the game. The "X's and O's"; the strategy, if you will. I also enjoyed the pure competitiveness of the sport. There is nothing like the sense of accomplishment shared with teammates after winning a game.

From day one, my coaches and mentors taught me the characteristics and the principles of being a good man, and understanding how to apply myself within the framework of good sportsmanship. They taught me what it takes to be strong through adversity. They taught me what it takes to be successful as an athlete and as a person. Working through pain is a key ingredient for success. I believe these characteristics are not only taught; they are also *learned*. It's important for people of influence to walk the walk, not just talk the talk, so that these young men and women can *see* it, not just *hear* it. I am grateful to have had many examples of people in my life who truly "walked the walk," Little did I know it at the time, but there would come many moments in the days ahead that I would draw strength from those examples and lessons.

I was lucky enough to grow up in a close family. My dad would take the time out of his busy day to coach me, and to teach me how to be the best athlete and person I could be. He never allowed much room for excuses, and held my older brother, Wes, and me accountable for our actions and decisions. Most of all, he taught us to only worry about what we could control, and never ever allow anyone to outwork us. Wes was my role model, and I can honestly say there is no better man who could have served in this role.

I am fortunate to have had many great, and I am very grateful for that, but of all these people and family members, I probably learned the most from my great-aunt and great-grandmother. I spent a lot of time with them, along with my grandmother and step-grandfather at a young age. That experience built a strong foundation for me. They helped me learn what inherent goodness is, where my faith should be placed, and what unconditional love is. All these traits that I observed and learned growing up helped me to develop, and shaped me into the person I am today.

My college career at Auburn University had its ups and downs on a team level and on a personal level. I came to Auburn with high expectations of my team and myself. I was blessed to be on the 2010 national championship team, which was an amazing experience. That set the bar high for my teammates and me. The next year (2011), I earned the starting job as the middle linebacker. I worked hard for this position and sacrificed a lot. It was all worth it because it was always a dream of mine to play in the SEC and at Auburn; starting in only your second year is a big deal.

We were one of the youngest teams in college football. That translated onto the field when we only won eight games that year. Coming off a national championship season, that was a big drop. But we never gave up. Our coaches even told us during the year that when adversity presented itself, we never once gave in. We kept fighting to the last play. In addition, we played an awful lot of snaps on defense, especially early in the season, averaging around ninety snaps per game; I rarely left the field. As a result, injuries began to set in, and by mid-season I was playing with high-ankle sprains on both ankles, a torn bicep, and a broken wrist that was in a cast.

Clearly, that impacted my performance, and ultimately my confidence to some extent. In retrospect, I probably shouldn't have been playing some of those games, but I don't regret it. At the time, I felt the team needed me and, quite frankly, pressing on is just part of who I am. It's in my DNA. We finished that season with a win over Virginia in the Chick-fil-a Bowl game. Personally, the fall of 2011 was a lot to handle because it was my first year to truly play as a starter in a key position in front of 85,000-plus people. It was a tough mental juggle between football and school studies. Majoring in building science, combined with having to deal with the mental side of leading a defense, was my first experience in dealing with such limited, tight, and stressful time constraints. It was definitely the most challenging year for me at Auburn on many levels, but as a result I also grew the most as an individual during that period.

The following year, 2012, was by far the most difficult season I'd ever been involved with at any level of football. After only winning eight games the previous season, we immediately went to work in the offseason. We put in countless hours in the weight room. With the new staff, we spent untold hours in the classroom learning a very complex defense and the completely different, pro-style offense that was to be implemented.

Even with all that hard work, the result was a record that turned out to be one of the worst years in Auburn football history. We faced a lot of adversity that season as a team. Toward the end of the season, our sense of belief in ourselves seemed to have vanished. Ultimately, we lost our head coach and staff.

On a personal level, a lot of individual criticism was targeted toward me. Most of it came through social media and message boards, with people blasting my name. This was a very hard time in my life. I had to wake up every day that season knowing people were looking down at me as though I was nothing, like I didn't belong there. I received daily hate messages on Twitter, Facebook, and sometimes even in person. It was decision time for me in a lot of ways. A gut check, if you will, on a very personal level. I decided to simply refuse to allow any of that to bring me down. I turned to God to give me guidance. I leaned on the people close to me. I remembered what my former coaches taught me about how to push through the pain. I learned that this didn't apply to just physical pain, but to emotional pain as well. I told myself that I wouldn't let what other people say and think control what I do with my life.

I basically ignored everyone who had something negative to say. I surrounded myself with people who truly cared about me. I put up a wall emotionally, and kept pushing for success in a season that seemed as though at the time there was nothing to be gained. I chose to play every minute as hard as I could, regardless of the outcome of the game. I later realized that all the ignorant criticism was only preparing me for the future.

In the 2013 offseason we, as a team, were determined and committed to getting better. We worked harder in the weight room to become stronger and faster. Again, we had a staff change and they brought in new systems. To our advantage, it was not as complicated as the previous system. We had learned so much conceptually from the old staff that the new system came relatively easy to us defensively. Offensively, most of the players remembered coach Malzahn's system from before, when he was the coordinator. Mentally, we were able to pick it all up more quickly than in the past season. This allowed us to focus on our physical play even more, and to become better individual players; that made the team as a whole much stronger.

We had more leadership on this team, which brought us together and helped us play as a unit. Overall, this was a much better team, even though it was made up of mostly the same players. It was definitely "a new day," and I will always appreciate coach Malzahn, coach Russell, and the rest of the staff for embracing a philosophy of team leadership through the players, and fostering an environment that enabled us to be successful. They trusted us, the seniors. We were able to take our hard work and win the first three games of the season. This was a big turnaround from the previous season. We went into the fourth game against LSU undefeated, and with a high confidence level. But we dug ourselves a hole early on and fell short of a win.

I remember how, after that game, we were mad and upset we didn't beat them because we knew we were the better team. The one thing that stuck out, though—the new difference—was that no one was hanging his head. As a team, we knew that we were good enough to accomplish something great and that we wouldn't let this one loss define our season. What did we do? We went back to work as if we had just won that game. We had the same desire and motivation to win the rest of our games. With that motivation, we were able to beat Georgia and Alabama in a glorious fashion. Those wins gave us the opportunity to become SEC champions and we did. Auburn needed this, and we did, too. It was the greatest turnaround in college football history, and I am forever grateful to have had an opportunity to be a part of that. It was a terrific way to end my career on the Plains.

The 2013 season was not all positive for me, however. At this point in my career, some of the negativity spewed my way earlier on the Internet sites, social media and so forth, had lingered and taken on a life of its own. I think some people had seen so much bad information that it was often accepted as truth. It was an unenviable position for me in that nothing I could do or say could change the repercussions of the assault on me as a player by some. Unfortunately, we as players are not immune to, nor insulated from, outside rhetoric. As a leader, you want to earn and gain the respect of your teammates. I'd always had that. But in 2013 it was a more difficult task because some of my teammates were hearing from other people that I "wasn't good enough." They were hearing and seeing the negativity. This made it almost impossible for me to gain the respect across the board I had put so much effort into achieving. It sometimes seemed that my efforts were futile. I again leaned on the people close to me. I prayed for guidance, and I kept pushing toward my goals and the team's goals. I vividly remember the first time they called out my name out over the loudspeakers as a starter back in 2011. It pumped me up. It made me feel great. It was a dream come true. Then, during the 2013 season, I remember the times my name would get called out before home games—my senior year—and the crowd, or at least the student section, would boo. I would ignore this to the best of my ability. I would even laugh it off sometimes, because I knew that they would have given anything to be in my shoes and to be able to play on that field. But the hard truth is, that was very tough. It wasn't the boos and it wasn't necessarily the criticism that bothered me. It was knowing that my teammates, the guys I was working so hard to earn respect from, my brothers, were also hearing that. Nonetheless, I knew that I had a job to do, and that was to do everything I could to help Auburn win. It wasn't for me. It wasn't for my family. It was for my God and for Auburn. I wanted to be able to say that I helped contribute to something greater.

Coach Gene Chizik always told us, "No matter who you are, no matter what kind of player you are, Auburn is bigger than you. Auburn was here before you, and will be here after you." I truly believed that, and still do today. Did I want my picture to one day be hanging from the stadium? Of course I did. Did I want people to speak my name with honor? Who doesn't? What made it even tougher was that people weren't just disgracing my name, they were also disgracing my father's name, my brother's name, my sister's name, and my mother's and my family's name. I know that it was very tough for them, as well, but I continued to lean on them for support. My family was strong and unwavering. They stood with me. I also showed them that I was tough throughout the process. Nothing anyone could say could change the man that I am: the man that they had raised, and the brother they grew up with. In the end, all of that served to make me stronger. I won because I never gave in. I never lost sight of the goal, and I never lowered my standards. I never let my school, my teammates, my family, or my coaches down. Not once. Was it easy? No, it wasn't. Nothing worthwhile ever really is.

At the end of the day, I grew stronger from this journey. I believe I am a better Auburn man than I would have been had it been an easier road. I was a three-year starter in a four-year career. I was chosen as that by three different defensive coordinators, three different position coaches and two different head coaches over a three-year span. I know that I earned it. I know that God has a plan for me, and that He guided me through adversity so that I would be better prepared for what lies ahead. I trust Him and I trust that plan. I look at this experience as an accomplishment through taking a road less travelled. I achieved and grew so much during my time at Auburn. I made lifelong friends, learned from some great people, and believe that I represented Auburn with honor and integrity. I am as proud as anyone ever has been to have worn that Orange and Blue. It's truly a unique privilege and honor. I now know that any obstacle I come across in life, I can overcome it. The process sharpened me, and I am grateful for the opportunity. Was it all worth it? You better believe it was!

War Eagle!

CHAPTER TEN

Learning How to Win

The meaning of football in the South is no secret, particularly football in the state of Alabama. As a young boy growing up in the suburbs of Birmingham, the importance of football to the culture I was raised in could not escape me. It was far more than entertainment; it was an identity, a year-round devotion and allegiance to the sport, the preparation it took to succeed, the sacrifices required for victory. I began learning these principles at age five at Center Point Ballpark.

My Little League team (this wasn't Little League as in the organization, but rather just peewee football), the Center Point Gators, won every game we played in five seasons, except for two very close losses. Those losses were both avenged in the playoffs or championship games those years. We won the state championship every year. We traveled to Florida to play the best teams in the South during the Thanksgiving holidays and beat all challengers. It was a lesson in learning how to humbly handle success, and a lesson that has served me well in life.

We hear often that losing builds character and I would agree. Losing highlights areas that need to improve. Losing shows us that things don't always go as planned; the hard work sometimes results in outcomes we dislike or did not expect. Losing forces us to change tactics, work harder, play smarter, make adjustments to alter the plan. Losing both builds and reveals character, as tough times draw out our innermost thoughts and actions. The real person surfaces when times are poor.

We don't hear it as often, but *winning* also builds and reveals character. Success in a sport or competition can certainly help shape the psyche of the competitor. It validates the effort exerted and makes the grind worthwhile. It motivates when the sacrifices required for success seem unendurable or futile. The winner has a choice to make: establish a tone and attitude of humility, or display a garish posture off-putting and belittling to your opponent and those witnessing your response. My Little League experience gave me ample opportunity to select and display one of these two character traits, and I am grateful for parents and coaches who taught the value, and demanded the response, of humility.

Unfortunately, my Auburn career didn't call for a victor's humility as often as did my Little League experience. Playing on two teams that won the western division of the Southeastern Conference, as well as two teams with losing records, my teammates and I had a sufficient number of opportunities to both win and lose well. Losing always hurt, always angered, always frustrated, but losing poorly was an embarrassment. I could live with giving my all and coming up short. I resented coming up short and making excuses, pointing fingers, or deprecating the victor. It's undoubtedly a learned process to handle losing with dignity and class. And we all wish we had fewer occasions to perfect the response.

But the experience of losing well comes in handy when, instead of losing a game, it is losing a spouse, a child, a marriage, a job, a home. No, these losses do not equate with merely losing a sporting event. The principle, however, still applies. How do you respond during difficult times? Character is built and revealed.

Winning in life is in the eye of the beholder. It means different things to different people, based on any number of disparate factors held in high regard by the individual. Some view winning as owning a house in the best neighborhood. Some see it as corporate superstardom. Some desire robotic children as idolatrous replicas of themselves; steering, goading, prodding their mini-mes toward careers and relationships that most benefit parent, not child.

For me, winning in life is found in having peace. Peace comes from recognizing I was not designed to handle life alone; I should quit trying to tackle life my way. I would do well to give up pursuing perfection and learn that contentment is a powerful virtue. Living life to please, appease, perfect, and perform for others is draining. Winning is not about how others perceive me, but how I am perceived by my Lord. And the Bible is clear: I am His, I am never alone, I will never be forsaken, all things work together for the good of those called according to His purposes.

Billy Graham states it best, "How does God define success? His measure is very different from the world's measure, and it can be summed in one sentence: Success in God's eyes is faithfulness to His calling. Paul was a failure in the world's eyes—but not to God. Even Jesus was a failure as far as most people were concerned, but 'he was faithful to the one who appointed him'—and that is all that mattered."

Sports taught me that failure is inevitable and will come despite my best efforts to tame. Sports taught that winning is worth the sacrifice and effort, making the exertion worthwhile. Sports taught humility in victory, because you remember the feeling of defeat. Learning to win is only impactful when there is a loser. In this new age world of "everyone wins, nobody fails, we all get a prize"—we are not teaching kids how to be winners. We are instead setting them up for failure. It's the experience of losing that provides the impetus to work harder, dig deeper, keep striving in an effort to avoid the disgust of defeat. Kids who never lose do not truly ever learn how to win. It is within the valleys we seek to obtain the mountaintops, and from the mountaintop you learn to appreciate and be content with your lot, having spent time in the valleys.

CHAPTER ELEVEN

Learning How to Lose: Dealing with Disappointment

Losing well is a lost art. In an ever-softening, offend-no-one, everyone-gets-a-trophy society, learning to deal with the real-world reality of failure is something we are failing to adequately teach our children. We want to protect them. We want to provide smooth sailing and make life easy for them. The payout initially is peace and contentment. The long-term result is an individual poorly equipped to handle the difficulties this world and life will certainly bring. My athletic upbringing taught me early the valuable messages of dealing with disappointment, learning how to lose the right way, experiencing failure, yet utilizing that moment as a building block, rather than as a ball and chain. Losing is never fun, and I don't advocate for complacency and acceptance of mediocrity. Whatever task you take up, whatever skill set has been bestowed on you, developing and honing those traits to maximize success is a noble effort. You are never stagnant in any area of your life. Mentally, physically, spiritually, emotionally, your relationships with your spouse, children, friends, coworkers, your God—you are either growing closer to one another or growing further apart. You are getting stronger or weaker. You are building intellect or it is fading. It's a moving scale in one direction or the other, but it never remains static.

Growing up the second of three boys, the competitive nature of sibling rivalry provided for me the initial exposure to falling short in competition. It's easier to lose the Iron Bowl than to lose a game of "twenty-one" on the basketball court, or even a "friendly" video game against a brother. Losing hurts. Losing to someone you see every day hurts worse. Losing to someone you share a home with hurts as bad as it gets. I learned early on that if I wanted to win against my brothers, if I wanted to bask in the ecstasy of victory, there would be a price to pay. I would have to practice and polish my skills. I had to figure out a strategy on the video game that was sound, a shot on the basketball court that could not be defended, a move with the football that was uncanny. If I wanted to be successful, I would have to be disciplined enough to work for the result.

Even so, sometimes I would still lose. I had put in the time and effort. I had practiced when no one was looking. I had prepared for the moment extensively, yet I found myself on the losing end. I'm thankful for those moments. I certainly wasn't thankful then. I am now. Losing to my brothers did not create a sense of poor self-worth, of feeling sorry for myself. It was a catalyst to improve. I hated the feeling of losing, and it sparked a renewed effort on my part to do whatever it took to not feel the sting of defeat again. It was a lesson in hard work, and it became ingrained in my character. If I wanted to win, I would have to outwork the competition.

More difficult than learning to rebound from a loss with an increased desire and intensity to train harder was learning to deal with an antagonistic sibling flaunting victory in your face. Figuring out how to be a good sport, to lose well, to be respectful in defeat, was certainly a learned behavior. It's why you can usually spot an only child with ease in early competition. They never lose because they seldom really compete. They don't experience the frustration and disappointment of defeat as often, making them novices on how to deal with the emotional surge. The more you experience the sting, the more you learn how to handle it. No, it never becomes easier. It's never a joy to walk off the field of play having lost. When it becomes easy to lose you should move on to something else; you no longer have the required passion needed to be relevant in your field. But the positive side of the coin is that learning to control your emotions and frustrations in losing such early competitions prepares you for the struggles that come later in life.

Athletics has provided the stage for me to learn the value of losing, and the character challenge to lose well. It provided the platform to take on the negatives that come with loss, and the learning that comes from dealing with that outcome. Sometimes I played on teams that lost in a hard-fought battle, neither team deserving to lose. Sometimes I lost on teams in humiliating fashion in a complete slaughter. Sometimes we lost due to self-inflicted errors or mistakes. Sometimes we lost due to poor coaching decisions or poor leadership. Sometimes we lost even though we were vastly superior in terms of talent. Sometimes we lost because we broke when adversity struck, or we weren't suited to play in an extreme environment. No matter how we lost, it always provided a significant lesson.

Sometimes in life you will outwork your competition, yet still lose the sale. Sometimes you will be equally matched, yet somehow unequally yoked in your level of successes. Sometimes you fail due to lack of preparation and due diligence. Sometimes you will stumble because of poor guidance, faulty leadership, hesitancy to make a difficult decision. Sometimes you will fail because the anxiety of a new surrounding or a difficult manager will topple a mentally weak individual. Athletics provided training in these scenarios for me. Athletes have a familiarity with life difficulties because such problems often translate from the field to the board room. It doesn't prepare you for everything, but it does teach you to be prepared for anything. It forces you to dig deep within yourself to find an inner strength to carry on. In individual sports *you* are all you have; you have no choice but to get back up and improve. In team sports, you have teammates counting on you and expecting you to do your part. To quit yourself would be to quit on your teammates.

And really, that it what sports *should* be all about. As great as it is to win, to win big and to win often, there is great value in *learning how to lose*. It's not an easy lesson to learn, but a necessity if one is to live a joyous life. Learning to lose well teaches self-control, humility, builds character, prepares you for the valleys in life. It also makes the successes taste that much sweeter.

Becoming a championship football team is a remarkably daunting achievement. Being part of the transformation into a championship football team a year removed from the abyss of defeat, demoralization, and disaster is sheer ecstasy. Why? Because the sting of the downfall is still fresh, and the exuberance of success yields a striking contrast. The difference between what it took to be a winner versus what you were doing as a loser is poignant because there is total recall. The change is palpable. It's a rare instance of seeing the product of "the reap and sow principle" so quickly. I lived this as an Auburn Tiger, going from an SEC title game to consecutive losing seasons, only to return to the SEC title game my senior season. The proverbial full circle.

Even more dramatic was the rise of the 2013 Auburn football team. SEC champions and seconds away from a national title only one season after going winless in conference play, losing its coaching staff, losing its desire to compete. The 2013 Auburn team was hardly the most talented. But they were hungry. They wanted to leave behind the feelings their disastrous 2012 season had aroused in them, and welcomed their new coaching staff overflowing with sound strategy, leadership, and discipline. The difference was stunning; so were the results. But having the past backdrop of a train-wreck season was what made the 2013 championship season that much more thrilling and satisfying.

I hope everyone reading this never has to fail. My wish is for the upmost success in all you attempt for a lifetime. The reality, however, is that you will experience some failure. We all do. That's life. Somewhere along the way, you will run up against a person, a technique, a position, a team, a force, a system for which you are no match. How will you respond? The answer to this question is what separates us. It's where the truly successful among us flourish. They have a plan. They have a grasp for what direction they will take should the initial approach come up short. They've been there and can draw from that experience. In my life, athletics provided this opportunity to learn to fail. And, because of the failure, the triumphs in life are more deeply appreciated.

Kendall Simmons is the quintessential "Southern gentleman." A warrior on the football field and a teddy bear off, Kendall is easily one of the nicest, most respectful people I have ever known. We entered Auburn as part of the same signing class, Kendall hailing from Ripley, Mississippi, choosing to spurn the state schools to become an Auburn Tiger. Kendall stands out to me as someone extremely familiar with two opposing characteristics in life and in athletics: he finds success in whatever he attempts even as physical challenges attempt to rob him of those successes. In short, he's learned to be a warrior off the field simply to survive unfortunate diagnoses. He is an inspiration to those who know him best, for his resolve to overcome injury and illness, and to not simply compete, but to excel at the highest levels.

Biography

The 30th pick of the 2002 NFL Draft, Kendall Simmons began his professional career with the Pittsburgh Steelers after a stellar but injury-hampered career at Auburn University. The Ripley, Mississippi, product, Kendall earned significant playing time as a true freshman along the offensive line, a rare feat in the trenches of the Southeastern Conference. A two-time first team All SEC selection and winner of the 2001 Jacobs Trophy given to the best blocker in each conference, Kendall was a dominant force playing multiple positions along the Auburn offensive front. A starter in eighty-three of the eighty-four NFL games he participated in, Kendall was a two-time Super Bowl winner and named to the 2002 NFL All Rookie Team. Injuries and illness were no stranger to Kendall, however, as he was forced to redshirt his junior season due to injuries sustained as a sophomore at Auburn. Multiple foot problems slowed Kendall for many years, and an Achilles tendon injury ended his 2008 season in Pittsburgh. His greatest challenge, which will continue for a lifetime, was a diabetes diagnosis early in his NFL career.

Living with Diabetes as a Professional Athlete

My name is Kendall Simmons, and my wife is Celesta Henry. We have three girls and a little boy. Kensley is ten, Laila seven, Olivia Pearl six, and Tyce two. I was blessed with the opportunity to play in the NFL for eight seasons. My life changed dramatically during the summer of 2003, heading into my second season with the Pittsburgh Steelers. Two-and-a-half weeks before training camp, I developed a lot of the symptoms related to the onset of diabetes. It started with fatigue, frequent trips to the restroom, extreme thirst, massive weight loss, and temporary vision loss. The time had come for me to leave for camp. The drive from Auburn to Pittsburgh was a challenge, as my symptoms got worse. I finally arrived in Pittsburgh and met with the head trainer, John Norwig, to explain to him how I felt. I was sent over to see Dr. Yates, one of the team doctors. Dr. Yates tested my blood glucose level, and immediately admitted me to the hospital. I had just turned twenty-three in March, and now I'm lying here with temporary vision loss and 45 pounds lighter. The following morning, my wife showed up to hear the life-changing news.

I was diagnosed with Type 1.5 or L.A.D.A. (Latent Autoimmune Diabetes of Adulthood) which falls into one of the different types of diabetes. This is the honeymoon phase before it evolves to Type 1.

Diabetes in today's world is classified as a silent killer. There are several different types of diabetes. Type 1, Type 2 and Gestational diabetes are the ones commonly known by the public. Diabetes has been a part of my life for eleven years. The mental and physical challenges diabetes presented every day for me as an athlete pushed me harder than sports ever did in my entire life. During the last seven seasons of my career, I never played a game when I felt perfect. The roller-coaster ride of diabetes affected every mental and physical snap I took in the NFL. I had to undergo thirteen surgeries during my football career. There were times during the off-season when I had multiple surgeries. I've always felt as though I was fighting an uphill battle.

People who live with diabetes heal more slowly than everyone else. Diabetes has an effect on every aspect of your life, but it can be managed. You have to make the decision to commit to your health. A good support group is key to successful diabetes management. I wouldn't be where I am today without God, my family, and the Steelers. The Rooney Family owns the Steelers, and they also know how diabetes can change your life. They have two kids with this disease. The support they've shown me made my transition a lot easier. Support from the coaches, teammates, and community really laid the foundation for the next phase of my life.

I finally decided to retire in late 2009, and to my surprise God decided to alter my path one more time, which led me to become a National Spokesperson for Novo Nordisk, the number one diabetes company in the world. Living with diabetes changed my approach to the football field, and made me a smarter athlete when it comes to training and playing the game. Diabetes also taught me more about myself than sports ever did. The best part about the dramatic change in my life is that I get a chance to give back. The path I'm on now has improved my life, because God knows I wouldn't have been able to take proper care of myself without it.

CHAPTER TWELVE

Psychology of Success in Sports

Dominant teams have an intrinsic ability to recognize weakness in an opponent and exploit it. Highly successful teams in any sport bombard you with pressure, constantly force you to keep up, and ultimately drain you of your discipline to remain fundamentally sound, and thus your will to compete. Great teams and individuals are capable of elevating to another level—not only when challenges arise and an adequate response must be made, but also when victory is within eyeshot, they can taste it, and do what is needed to reach out and clutch it. These characteristics define the killer instinct in athletics. It represents the psychology of success in sport.

I've played on teams that were beaten before the game even began, simply because of our mind-set. Of course, in every athletic competition the ball bounces in unforeseen ways. You prepare for a zone defense, but get a heavy dose of man-on-man. You expect the right-handed junk-ball pitcher, only to get the left-handed flamethrower. Getting beat strategically or overpowered by superior athleticism is one thing. Losing before the game is played is quite another.

In high school we played the Mountain Brook Spartans all four years. Sometimes we had more talent and sometimes they were more skilled, but regardless of talent we were beaten soundly every single year. That entire week of pre-game practice had a unique feel of hopelessness. You could sense an entire team with little confidence things would go our way, even after beating highly ranked opponents the previous week. We did not enter with fire, or passion, or belief. We entered with automatic negative thoughts, fully expecting the worst to occur. Every year, the game was played in a monsoon. Every year, our play mirrored the weather—dastardly, uninspiring, sloppy. Every year, even winless, hapless, talent-starved Mountain Brook teams defeated us with ease. We were beaten before we ever teed it up. In fact, we were beaten the moment the schedule was released.

My last two seasons of high school, Mountain Brook was very good and should have beaten us. My first two seasons, Mountain Brook was below average, yet still had their way with us. Those games against Mountain Brook taught me a valuable lesson in life about the overwhelming power of negative thoughts, disbelief, hopelessness, and its downhill-snowball effect on mindset and results. When you enter with a defeatist's outlook, you will walk away the disheartened failure every single time.

My sophomore year at Auburn was similar, and just as deleterious to team morale and unity. Simply stated, our offense in 1998 at Auburn was atrocious. Partly due to injuries, partly youth, partly scheme, partly lacking in talent, and as the season progressed, totally lacking in belief in ourselves. Defensively, we entered each game waiting for the offense to implode, never to be disappointed. More times than not, the implosion was activated on the game's first drive.

When Tommy Tuberville took over as coach following that miserable 1998 season, he made two key moves that began to chip away at the cancer of negativity we as players were swimming in. He hired Kevin Yoxall as our strength and conditioning coach, instituting hard work, accountability, and toughness into the program, and for players in whom it had been was frighteningly absent. He also hired Chette Williams as our "spiritual coordinator," ushering in optimism, understanding, and appreciation of our teammates' personal stories, thus injecting grace, peace, and stability into our lives though a closer walk with God. What Coach Tuberville did was change our attitudes, our outlooks, our negative mindset, our psychology, into mentally tough brothers-in-arms, a team united in every way.

We all struggle with doubts, negative thoughts, anxieties, and inner turmoil. The things we worry about may be different, but we all have things that creep into our subconscious, and ultimately affect our persona. Sometimes our doubts are healthy, fueling a journey to find answers we desperately seek. Sometimes our fears and thoughts are unhealthy, because they paralyze our actions and hinder happiness and peace. Just as this negative psychology infects an athletic squad, so, too, will it crush our spirits in all avenues of life. It permeates and afflicts all whom we touch, because it becomes our sole obsession. We begin to bow down to the doubt until it defines who we are. That is no way to live life. Overcoming the onslaught of automatic negative thinking requires vigilance and fight. It requires fighting a powerful force with an even mightier weapon. It's the realization that we don't have to do battle all alone; in fact, we were not made to journey through life independently. In sports we lean on teammates, coaches, trainers, and supporters. In life we lean on our spouse, our families, our friends, our neighbors, our church leaders, our community groups. In the Christian faith we lean on the God of the universe through Jesus Christ via an eternal, personal relationship with a God who knows the number of hairs upon our heads (or freckles on our skin for the hairless!). It is through communion with others that we reach our full potential in almost every life endeavor. That is the beauty of team sports. You never go it alone. You walk into adverse, raucous, intimidating environments linked arm in arm with a brother you'd give your life for. More times than not, that brother is of a different race, a different rung on the socioeconomic ladder, a confidant society would shun or think less of, or attempt to separate and divide from you on the basis of dissimilarities.

The sense of brotherhood is the positive psychology that pervaded my upbringing in sports, and is easily one of the greatest treasures in my life: the feeling of unity and belief in my teammates, our plan, our preparation, our ability to get the job done together. When prognosticators, talking heads, and even our own families, believed triumph was futile, we believed in each other. The result was not always favorable, but when our mentality was healthy the belief was certainly there, and that is what was most important. No hope equates to no chance. No belief links to universal disappointment—one of life's few guarantees.

Your mind is powerful. Reduced to its simplest form, your mind is in constant battle, a struggle between a positive outlook and a negative viewpoint. Experiences, genetics, personalities, surroundings are all factors in shaping our thoughts. Fight the battle with additional forces. Use all the help that surrounds you. Internal drive, responsibility, and courage are respectable traits we hold in high esteem. Adding the layer of connection, openness, and willingness to let others come alongside and support our efforts, whether physically, emotionally, or spiritually, can often be the missing ingredient in a positive outlook and a hopeful nature.

I knew Heath Evans was unique the very first time we met. As members of the same 1997 Auburn freshman signing class, Heath and I were polar opposites, yet alike at the same time. We were white guys who played positions dominated by blacks. We were both firm in our Christianity, yet failed to live up to Christ's standard every day. Heath was extroverted, an open book who attended private school in West Palm Beach. I was a thinker, more reserved, much more resistant to welcoming others into my inner circle of friends, and attended county school in the middle-class Birmingham suburbs. Heath combined size with speed like few others, and utilized his strengths to maintain a decade-long NFL career, playing on some great teams along the way. Heath knows what it takes to be successful in sports at the highest level, and utilizes the methods and teachings he acquired along the way, specifically the "Belichick Way," in all of his life endeavors.

Biography

Super Bowl XLIV champion Heath Evans serves as an analyst for numerous NFL Network programs.

Evans is seen regularly weekdays on Total Access, is known for his sharp wit and honest commentary, and has never had a problem speaking his mind. Prior to landing at the NFL Network, Heath enjoyed a stellar ten-year NFL career, capped by a Super Bowl Championship in 2010 with the New Orleans Saints, Super Bowl XLIV. He was the first fullback taken in the 2001 draft, selected by the Seattle Seahawks in the third round, the 82nd overall pick. In addition to the Seahawks and Saints, Heath played for the New England Patriots and Miami Dolphins.

A native of Florida, Heath was drafted by the NFL out of Auburn University. He averaged more than four yards per carry as a running back for the Tigers. He was a two-time All-State high school tailback in West Palm Beach. Today, Heath resides in Southern California with his wife and two daughters.

In addition to working at the NFL Network, Heath is a game analyst for the NFL on FOX. He never gets tired of talking football, and was tutored by two of the game's best coaches, Bill Belichick and Sean Payton.

Over the duration of his career, Heath lent his name to several causes and community efforts. He is the founder of the Heath Evans Foundation, an organization that raises support and awareness for abused children.

In the offseason, he also travels the country delivering motivational speeches. He once told a group, "The game of football has taught me many valuable life lessons that I feel I have a duty to share with others because of the platform the NFL shield has given me. I firmly believe in the willingness to open up about my mistakes, as much so, if not more than, my successes. I believe humility is a man's greatest strengths, and all championship teams, successful businesses, or exceptional people, are built with humility at their core."[1]

---

[1]www.nfl.com

Coaching: The Ability to Cripple or Create

By Heath Evans

I've had many coaches. Nine different head football coaches, from high school through the NFL. They all had their own styles, and they all had their own belief systems of how to best build a team, but one in my mind was the best way:

The Patriot Way! Or, as I know it to be—"the Belichick Way!"

The Belichick Way could also be described as:

- The Selfless Way
- The Overly Prepared Way
- The Humble Way
- The Put the Team First Way
- The Do your Job Way

No matter where I go, football fans always ask one of two questions:

1) What makes Bill Belichick so different?
2) How are his teams so good every year?

The answer is the same for both questions.

My answer always leaves the fans wanting more, or sometimes even disappointed, because they expect some magical response or formula for Belichick's success. The answer is simple, yet what gives Bill the ability to pull off—what he is so uniquely gifted at—is mostly God-given, in my opinion. His ability to see into a player's physical makeup, but, more importantly, mental and emotional makeup is a true gift! A knack—and it can't be replicated. Bill sets a priority on physical and mental toughness over athletic ability. Of course, great talent is needed to achieve success at any level of sports, or business for that matter, but Bill's ability to see and sense a player's mental makeup is what sets him apart.

Yes, he has a unique ability for developing great talent whom many others have passed on, but his true giftedness shows up in knowing how to push, prod, and sometimes humiliate, all types of different personalities and players, to gauge how they will react and respond in any given football situation. What always intrigued me the most about Bill was that he was always much more concerned about the players' *later* response to the pushing and prodding than their initial reaction to the criticism. Bill wanted to see how the player handled the initial criticism, but he was much more focused on whether or not the player was able to digest the coaching given, and not make the same mistake twice. Or whether he could implement the coaching given next time, when he was pressed into that situation again.

Most coaches will let the better athlete get away with more deficiencies in areas of mental and physical toughness. Not Bill! Every player is attacked differently, but with the same level of demand. Actually, I would say the so-called super star players are coached even harder than the fifty-third man on the roster, and that is a true rarity. And to go back a sentence—I didn't use the word "attacked" by chance. There is a concerted effort on Bill's part to diagnose and establish what every player's strengths and weakness are. Yes, physically, but more importantly mentally and emotionally.

Probably the most important thing I learned in my four seasons under Bill is that the mental and emotional strengths of a player are by far the most important aspects of the game of football. Everyone can imagine the stresses of playing an NFL game in front of 80,000-plus in the stands and millions more watching at home. How a player reacts to that stressful environment is one thing, but most players have already experienced that these days, when some college programs are even more visible than some NFL teams.

Bill is trying to diagnose the mental capabilities of the player to take moment by moment, in-game coaching, and be able implement it immediately as if he had practiced it all week. Imagine a player being prepped all week for a certain type of game plan that was based on what another team has previously done. You then get into that particular game, and the game plan that had been strategized turns out not to be what is needed to win the game. The ability to improvise and adjust parts, if not the whole game plan, and then execute it as if you had practiced it all week is what Bill looks for in the players he keeps on his roster.

Obviously, these types of situations have the potential to create great emotional stress on the player but also to demand a level of mental capability that is rare in a collection of athletes. This is the type of mental toughness that is demanded from Bill. Week in and week out, players are forced to learn a new offense or defense that best gives the team the ability to win. Most teams are game plan–driven each week, but at the core there are few changes made to the basic offense or defense. Under Belichick, almost every week you will see a unique approach to how the offensive and defensive staffs are attacking their upcoming opponent. This can't happen without players who aren't capable of handling the cerebral challenges that come with such significant changes week to week.

Part one of the answer to why Bill's teams are great year in and year out is because he will always take the lesser athlete who is *mentally* tougher over the better athlete who is lacking in the mental toughness department. What does mental toughness mean? My best attempt to sum up how Coach Belichick would define mental toughness would be this: can you be counted on to do your job when the pressure and stakes are at their highest? If the answer in Bill's mind is yes, you are mentally tough.

The second part of the answer is physical toughness. There is a sign hanging in the training room in New England that says, "Durability Is More Important than Ability." This speaks to the core of the physical toughness that Bill demands from his players. Most teams are full of physically strong guys, but I think toughness is displayed in a variety of ways that differs from simply being physically strong. Toughness can make a good athlete a great athlete. There is no other sport that puts you in as many uncomfortable situations as does the game of football. After the first practice of the season, you are never 100 percent healthy again, so for the next twenty-plus weeks of the NFL season you are faced with the question,"Does my body control me, or do I control my body?"

There are many strong athletes who are not tough enough to push their own bodies through the demanding grind of an NFL season. They are the players who believe they can coast through practice, or skip a practice, because they just don't feel quite up to it. They don't see the value of sacrificing their bodies for the betterment of the team, or for their own game preparation. These principles certainly tie into the mental toughness department, but are very different. You have many tough guys who could play through a variety of injuries that would sideline most others, but they are missing the intelligence factor, the cerebral component of mental toughness. You also have players who are extremely smart, and who thrive under the brightest of lights with maximum pressure, but having to battle through nagging injuries that other teammates could handle forces them out of competition. Perhaps they bow out for personal protection reasons, or just because they cannot tolerate the discomfort of playing through an injury that shouldn't sideline them. Either way, it reflects the fact that they are not willing to do what is best for the team. Those players don't last very long under the Belichick way.

The simple answer to the question of Bill's success is that he sees the value in the lesser athlete that who will daily lay it on the line for the betterment of the team, and be fully accountable for his actions on and off the field. He knows that guy will be prepped and ready for every situation possible, because he has made the necessary sacrifices to be primed for the moment. The proof is in the results. It's the Belichick way: choosing the lesser athlete who is physically and mentally tough over the spectacular athlete who lacks those qualities, or who cares only about himself, his brand, or his stats.

I titled this "Coaching: The Power to Cripple or Create" because that is the tremendous power of a coach. Coaches have the power to hurt and harm or build up and strengthen an athlete. I've had a few who probably unknowingly hurt me far more than they helped me, but for four seasons in New England I saw the Belichick way create many a great football player. The sad part is, there could have been so many more if they would have just bought into Bill's system. So many young, talented players and even well-established NFL stars refused to humble themselves and submit to the Belichick way, and they ultimately crippled themselves.

At the heart of everything Bill does lies the question, "What is best for the team?" Not what makes Bill look the best? Not what gets Brady the best stats? Not how does the coaching staff devise a scheme that gets them the glory? Not how do we keep the GM or owner happy? It's always what is best for the team. No individual in mind. Only the team.

What I have found outside and away from the game is that this is the recipe for success in anything. Find the group of individuals who could care less about personal acclaim and recognition. Find the people willing to follow a humble leader. Find the people who consistently do everything with only one question in mind: what is best for the team? If you do, in the end you will always produce a winner!

CHAPTER THIRTEEN

Faith in Sports

There is an old saying, "There are no atheists on a battlefield." Similarly, my experience in athletics, particularly football, has shown a significant reliance by players on the supernatural force of God the Creator. Whether it be a formal team prayer meeting the night before a game, a Fellowship of Christian Athletes (FCA) conference, a growing relationship with Jesus Christ through the trials and triumphs experienced in sport, pleading for mercy from injuries, or seeking to utilize to the fullest extent the platform athletics has bestowed, athletics and spirituality have a unique mesh point.

Perhaps the connection between religion and athletics stems primarily from my deep southern heritage. In the state of Alabama, college football is almost a religion all its own. The margin between athletics and faith was blurred quite often as the nature of the sport created circumstances conducive to spiritual growth. I had coaches who believed fervently in spiritual maturity as foundational to personal and team success. In fact, Coach Tommy Tuberville went so far as to hire Reverend

Chette Williams as a full-time pastor to shepherd the football team. Tuberville's sales approach to Chette was specific. He had an offensive coordinator and a defensive coordinator. What he needed now was a spiritual coordinator. Chette Williams was that man. What was a novel concept in 1999 has since become routine across college campuses in America. Why? Because athletics and faith go hand in hand.

I've always maintained that my most memorable moments as an Auburn Tiger took place far from the football field. What I treasured were the prayer meetings we had together as a team on Friday nights before games. They were always held in the offensive meeting room. They were always non-mandatory. They were always emotional, impactful, and stirring. Big, strong teammates brought to their knees through pain, family strife, injury, spiritual decay, frustration. In contrast, others joyous for new opportunities, blossoming relationships, births of children, success on the field or in the classroom. You found out weekly how little you actually knew the teammate you've bled with, fought for, and stood by for years. This wasn't a forced meeting by coaches or by a "spiritual coordinator." This was player—established and player-run. And, at the conclusion of my time as an Auburn Tiger, this non-mandatory, player-driven meeting was attended by all players and all coaches. Why? Because we grew closer to one another by growing closer to God. Because we needed an avenue to break down, and a pathway to mend. Because, again, athletics and faith go hand in hand.

I never walked off a football field, from age five as a Center Point Stallion to age twenty-two as a San Diego Charger, without praying at midfield at the game's conclusion. I never played in a football game in high school and college without a devotion the day prior to, or day of, the game. I prayed throughout every football game I ever played, sometimes pleading for energy and stamina, sometimes injury prevention, sometimes to win, sometimes for thanksgiving for the opportunity, sometimes to just finish in one piece. It was an epic dichotomy—the battle between the serenity and faith of being held tightly by your Creator juxtaposed against the brutality, viciousness, and hard attitude required to survive and thrive in an overly aggressive sport. Prayer throughout, combined with the trash-talking, foul-mouthed, vehement passion of an attacker.

Perhaps a large part of the spiritual awareness and presence within football is the need to bring balance to teams and individuals. Players and coaches alike are under tremendous pressure to win games. Many times, both succumb to those pressures with poor decision-making, poor habits, poor lifestyle choices, poor time management. In season, you're pulled to the extreme in so many areas: physical exhaustion from a season of pounding; a strength coach's demands; mental fatigue from game planning and film study, combined with classwork and the demands of a curriculum. There is little time to spend in reflection or meditation, to take a spiritual sabbatical, to maintain a Bible reading track, or to attend church services regularly. In fact, many teams, including my teams at Auburn, had meetings, weight-lifting, and practice on Sundays, all preventing church attendance. Our days off on the practice fields were Mondays.[1]

Corporate worship with a church family was difficult to maintain during the season. That made prayer meetings and worship together as a team all the more important and

[1]I always thought it was crazy to hold practice and meetings on Sundays. Game time and time of arrival home in Auburn after a road trip mattered not. Play the late ESPN game in Baton Rouge and finish around 10 p.m. Shower, interview, visit family, and travel to airport. Fly from Baton Rouge to Montgomery. Bus from Montgomery to Auburn. Arrive in Auburn at 3 a.m. See you at the athletic complex in the morning at eleven for meetings. God forbid you get banged up in the game. See you in the training room at eight.

powerful. It provided the equilibrium we missed in our lives because of a demanding schedule. It provided the pause we all needed in a world that never stops. It provided the opportunity to reflect on, and give praise for, gifts and platforms given to us that others work so hard to obtain, yet often never see come to fruition.

It is already quite a humbling experience to play major college football, to become a part of something so uniquely important and meaningful in the lives of so many. It is also a humbling experience to take yourself out of the center of the universe, and replace it with the Creator. In the world of an elite athlete competing before millions, sometimes that gets lost. God is not the center of your universe; your sport is, your time is, your body is. In reality, you place yourself squarely in the center. Having a pathway back to align your walk biblically is vital in athletics. I was fortunate to have coaches, at all levels, who not only recognized this, but lived it.

There's a reason why a non-mandatory prayer meeting had 100 percent attendance, and the attention of all there. There's a reason several teammates were baptized at a local church by our team chaplain, to the delight of the team. There's a reason Auburn football underwent a renaissance midway through the 1999 season, catapulting the program toward sustained success. The reason was unity. Unity arrived through prayer. Being humble enough to display weaknesses. Humble enough to say aloud that you didn't have all the answers, and to bow to the One who does. Humble enough to recognize that the things you say, and the manner in which you act, impacts those around you. Humility and togetherness triumphing over individualism, selfishness. That's the story of rebirth in my life, and in the life of my football team at Auburn. Faith and sports, it's a powerful combination. A life-altering experience.

I have known and admired Jason Standridge for almost my entire life. We grew up together playing football and baseball at Center Point Ball Park in Birmingham, AL. Even as kids, Jason possessed the type of charisma and "aw-shucks" persona that made everyone around him feel comfortable and truly a friend. A person of deep-seated Christian faith, Jason was Tim Tebow before Tim Tebow, a handsome, stellar athlete, passionate about Christ and seemingly unaware of the aura he possesses. Jason and I went to rival high schools and flourished athletically. We roomed together on our official visit to Auburn, and were going to room together as freshmen. He, however, became a near millionaire right after graduation, and chose the baseball route over football. He is a great man, and I'm proud to call him a friend.

Biography

Jason Standridge was born November 9, 1978, in Birmingham, AL. Having played professional baseball as a pitcher since being drafted in the first round as a senior in high school in 1997, Jason currently plays for the Fukuoka Softbank Hawks in Japan. As the state's top ranked quarterback coming out of high school, Jason accepted a football scholarship to Auburn University; however, a professional baseball career was the route he chose. Jason has pitched for numerous organizations in his MLB career, including the Tampa Bay Devil Rays, Texas Rangers, Cincinnati Reds, and the Kansas City Royals, as well as the Hanshin Tigers and Fukuoka Softbank Hawks in the Japanese league. Jason is married to his wife, Joy, and has two children, with a third on the way as of this writing.

How Athletic Principles Have Strengthened My Faith

By Jason Standridge

You hear the old cliché, "practice makes perfect!" Well, I wish I could have a talk with the fella who came up with that analogy, because it doesn't work like that. Athletes aren't perfect. Never will be. As a professional baseball player, I can't recall too many times when I've even been *close* to perfect over my eighteen-year career. As a matter of fact, my faith isn't perfect either. But there are some principles I've learned over the years, through my athletic life, that have served me well in my spiritual life.

"Christian athletes are just not tough."
"Christian athletes can't be mean on the football field."
"Christian athletes are just too soft."

If you're a Christian and play sports, you might have heard these phrases. I've heard them many times, and it makes me want to put my fist through a wall! Well, not exactly, but it does make me upset.

My relationship with Jesus defines who I am. It allows me to live a freed-up life without worrying about problems or situations that arise in my journey. This isn't a nonchalant attitude that many Christian athletes get labeled with. Instead, it's a my-self-worth-comes-from-Jesus-attitude. When I make a mistake, I learn from it, and don't let it scare me into making another one. That's because of my confidence. I'm secure in who I am. My statistics on the baseball field *do not* define me.

In baseball, everything is calculated by numbers. There's a statistic for everything. In a sense, it reveals the player you are. What you're worth on a baseball field is defined by the statistics you produce. This is tough, and at times is a cruel reality. But It can also be a blessing. I've been on both sides of the spectrum. Teams can love you one year, and in the next look for your replacement.

In the sports world, failure is part of the gig. Baseball is even more extreme. A player can have a .300 batting average and be called great, even a Hall of Famer. But what you don't realize is that it means he is failing 70 percent of the time! That's a pretty poor success rate. If you took a 70 percent failure rate into your next job, you'd probably be job hunting again very shortly.

These are lessons you learn to deal with. I hate to lose. I don't even want to lose at *checkers*! But, failure is inevitable, and you learn to process it. It's what we do with that failure that's important.

How do you handle failure?
Does it make you want to quit?
Or does it make you want to become better, and not experience that loss again?

In my career, I've had many struggles and failures. I've been told I wasn't good enough, and told I wasn't needed. I've also been encouraged and told I *was* good, and that gave me confidence. Confidence breeds success. Success breeds confidence. But in order to have confidence, you must have something to draw from. In my case, in the case of a Christian athlete, that source you draw from is God's word, the Bible.

Now, let me stop here and be clear about something.

Many people would argue about bringing God into a sporting event. Many people have asked me, "If there are two Christian athletes opposing each other, who wins?" Great question, because it's our human nature to believe that the one that is "the better Christian" would win. God doesn't work like that. God is not interested in who wins and losses as much as He's interested in how we handle the outcome. It's about Him. Wins glorify self. Losses glorify no one, but make you pray for more wins or success. Funny, but true.

So am I saying we should lose to be in constant communion with God? Well, no! God wants us to do our best and to succeed, but as long as it glorifies Him. If we start believing that our wins or success in life are from our hard work or effort, then we have lost sight of our goal. My goal is to glorify God with the talent He's given me. If that means I win, then all the glory goes to Him. Same as a loss. What I've found out over the years is that He shows me so much more about my relationship with Him through failure or losses than through wins. God allows failure in our lives to help us grow and learn.

I've pitched in some important games in my career, and have failed miserably in some of them. People will watch how you deal with failure. It is imperative that we stay mindful of this. I have thrown things and pitched a fit after a loss. I've also sat quietly and cheered for my teammates. Both examples expose you. Believe me, the latter reaction will serve you well, and you will honestly be liked more. The point is simple. How you handle your failure reflects how you ultimately view God. And if you view God as a cosmic Santa Claus who is ready to put you on the naughty list, or zap you every time you mess up, well, failure will continue to eat you alive.

Never be afraid to fail. I have a six-year-old son, and I am constantly reminding him, "Don't be afraid to fail." Why do I say that? It's simple. Life is full of failures, and failure makes you want to give up. You never know how good you can be unless you try, and still fail. And I never want my son to be scared of trying something because he thinks he's going to fail and not be good enough. We will fail. Don't sit in it. I've heard the story of Thomas Edison after he invented the light bulb. He was praised and asked how he discovered the invention. His response: "I didn't just find the way to invent the light, but thousands of ways *not* to!"

The Bible is full of truths and promises. John 15:4-8 says: "4 Remain in me, as I also remain in you. No branch can bear fruit by itself; it must remain in the vine. Neither can you bear fruit unless you remain in me.

"5 I am the vine; you are the branches. If you remain in me and I in you, you will bear much fruit; apart from me you can do nothing. 6 If you do not remain in me, you are like a branch

> *that is thrown away and withers; such branches are picked up, thrown into the fire and burned. 7 If you remain in me and my words remain in you, ask whatever you wish, and it will be done for you. 8 This is to my Father's glory, that you bear much fruit, showing yourselves to be my disciples."*

This is encouragement. This is our life source. It is essential that we understand how much truth this verse is. Jesus is telling us the key to our spiritual and physical lives. Encouragement, confidence and perseverance are necessary components to live a Godly life. But they also are mandatory for our normal everyday life. I've never met a person who doesn't want to be encouraged. Ever! I speak from experience on this. Whenever a coach or even a teammate comes up to me and gives me any sort of encouragement, there is something inside me that believes what he is saying. This gives me hope and confidence, which enables me to persevere through the tough times (or losses). This is what God's word does for us, too.

It is so easy to relate my athletic life to my spiritual life. I understand that I'm a sinner. Romans 3:23 says everyone has sinned and fallen short of God's standard. This is part of the failure I have to process in my spiritual life. I learn that God is molding me, and my journey is not over. If I was perfect, there wouldn't be any need of a savior. And I need a savior. I've lost many games in my career. I've failed and fallen short of my coaches' and managers' standards. I've even fallen short of the standards I set for myself on the field. I have to process the failure, and learn how it strengthens me into being a better player.

Pick yourself up, dust yourself off and keep going, What a concept! It's simple, but a little frustrating at times. Overcoming failure and persevering is what motivates me to continue to strive for excellence. Perfection? Ha! No such thing. But we should at least strive to be the best we can be. Excellence is an attitude of never giving up. I will never forget the words my dad would say to me when I was young. In anything I was doing, he would say, "Believe in yourself!" He gave me encouragement and confidence all the time. This allowed me to start believing what he said was true. If I believed in myself, that I could accomplish my goal, then I would never believe anything opposite of that to be true. This has been a staple in my life. Positive thinking will always lead to something positive.

Even if the results are negative, you will find something positive in them. In baseball, I have to believe that I'm better than my opponent. It's called a mental edge. If I believe a negative thought or result, even for only a second, I'm already beat mentally. I've lost the mental edge and given it to my opponent. If I can control those negative thoughts, and take a step back and counter those negatives with positives, then I'm ready to compete again. Sounds like a lot going on in an athlete's head, doesn't it? Well, you're right. It's part of the job, and it separates the good players from the mediocre ones.

This has translated to, and strengthened, my spiritual life. My faith is based on two true events: the death and resurrection of my savior, Jesus Christ. My salvation is in Him. Jesus says, "Believe in Me!" Just as I draw strength from my dad's words so long ago, I draw strength from these words even more. I believe in Jesus and He loves me no matter what I've done. 1 John 4:4 tells us, "*Greater is He that is in me, than he that is in the world.*" He lives in me and has overcome evil. I may fail and I may sin, but Jesus has already paid the price for my sins and failures. This allows me to pick myself up and keep striving for excellence. Keep pursuing God through the wins and losses in life. God never wants us to give up. When we feel weak and battered from life and from the enemy (Satan), we find courage to know that Jesus is carrying us through those times. It's never us who make it through. It's always Him right there with us.

Never be afraid to fail, because Jesus loves failures.

CHAPTER FOURTEEN

Timing

On every college campus where football is played, summer ushers in a "non-mandatory" practice period for quarterbacks and receivers. It is an opportunity to get in rhythm in the passing game, and to attempt to perfect timing between quarterback and receiver. It's of vital necessity, because when timing is not superb, neither is production. The most successful defenses in football garner their achievement by disturbing and stifling timing with mental and visual deception, aggressive press man coverage, a speedy, efficient pass rush. If a defense disrupts the timing of the offense, it has the upper hand.

Every sport operates this way. Timing is of the essence, whether it is your physical approach toward the net in tennis; your jump off the pitcher's movement while stealing second base, or even; where an opponent falls on the schedule as it relates to your own team's preparedness, or even when a key player misses a game because of injury. Timing makes a monumental difference in all we do athletically.

I watch my daughter daily practice gymnastics. Timing in gymnastics is critical, as the slightest movement, the smallest gesture, the most innocuous of miscues can have a profound impact on an apparatus score. Those girls are trained to perfect their timing, be it tumbling on the floor, launching to spring from the vault, or deciding when to release the bar to dismount.

In a myriad of life endeavors, timing is of critical importance. Events set into action a cause and effect motion, with ripples touching countless people for better or worse, results often directly correlating to the timing of the incident.

In 2001, I signed a one-year free agent contract with the San Diego Chargers, after completing my career as four-year starter at safety at Auburn University. I wasn't passionate about playing football in the NFL, but rather viewed the opportunity as the logical next step. I wanted to see if I could compete at the highest level. Unfortunately, my timing was poor on several fronts. First, an unresolved neuromuscular illness the summer prior to my final season at Auburn sent my draft stock tumbling southward. Clear MRIs, muscle-nerve conduction tests, muscle biopsies, and neurologist reports would not convince NFL teams I was 100 percent healthy. Had I entered the draft after my junior year, I would have been drafted, but now I was damaged goods. My timing was poor.

The Chargers were willing to give me a shot, having nothing to lose by taking a chance on me. They eyeballed me from afar and called that a physical, then signed me without any fanfare a few weeks after the draft. I would compete as one of more than one hundred men attempting to break into the fifty-three- man roster. The starter at my strong safety position was a Pro Bowl performer, the best in the league at his position, named Rodney Harrison. Rodney did his own thing; he practiced to the beat of his own drum. It was impossible to watch Rodney in practice and learn the safety responsibilities from him, because he played the position in a wholly unorthodox way, even calling me aside to tell me, "Don't emulate me if you want to make the team. These coaches won't let you get away with what I do!" He was a great player, a terrific person, a model teammate, but not the guy you want to see holding down your position as you are attempting to make an NFL squad. My timing was poor. Or was it?

Something I have found to be true, and believe with every ounce of my being, is that God's timing is always perfect. It certainly will not match up with what we believe is the perfect timing for our lives, but the God of the universe does not make mistakes nor mangle timelines. The events that led to my departure from football happened for reasons of God's choosing: to point me in a new direction in life. Although my passion to play football had dwindled, the desire to make a living and support my young family, the motivation to do the near impossible of making an NFL roster as an undrafted free agent, was a daily driving force. In my timeline, if I were writing my own story, I would have included an NFL career for financial gain, validation of my talent, and the satisfaction of proving doubters wrong.

Failure in one arena proved to be a launching pad to other goals and successes. School became a breeze without football dominating my time and energy. I was home with my wife and infant daughter, rather than across the country with air traffic grounded due to the September 11 terrorist attacks that altered the fabric of our nation. The experience of attempting something grand, but falling short, was in some ways liberating, displaying to me that it was far better to try and fail than to fail to try. And the frustration of feeling as if my timing was as poor as possible, in hindsight, appeared remarkably beneficial and even ingenious.

The importance of timing and the consequences of ill-timed actions are ingrained in the athlete. The perfectly timed blitz wreaks havoc on an unsuspecting offense; however, a poorly scheduled blitz is easily identified, easily accounted for, and places the defense at an immense disadvantage. The same players, same responsibilities, same technique, with totally different results based entirely on timing. The cancer diagnosis, the loss of employment, the natural disaster that destroys possessions are never in our own planned timing and wreak havoc on real people.

Our timelines would never include these terrible trials, yet God's timing allows for them. In hindsight, perhaps on the other side of eternity these afflictions will make sense and can be understood through the view of a far more powerful lens. On this side of eternity, however, we remain staggered and stunned by the timing of it all. God's word offers rest in that *"all things work together for the good of those that love the Lord and are called according to His purposes"* (Romans 8:28). For those who heed that message, the same diagnosis, the same loss of revenue, the same loss of possession does not equate to loss of identity nor loss of hope. Poor timing is in the eye of the beholder, and for the Christian, God Almighty's timing is perfect. Yes, we still grieve; yes, we still are angered; yes, we still struggle with the calamities of life on earth. But our hope rests in God's perfect timing.

Coach Eddie Gran came to Auburn with Coach Tommy Tuberville in 1999, my junior year, serving as running backs coach. The next season, he took on the additional responsibility of special teams coordinator. Being a defender, I had little interaction with Coach Gran beyond special teams work. I do, however, remember my teammate, Heath Evans, telling Coach Gran upon his arrival that he was the best tailback Coach Gran had on campus. Heath claims Coach Gran told him he'd never be a tailback, and backed up that assertion by placing Heath on the scout team defensive line for several weeks. Heath saw zero carries until injuries decimated our running backs corps to the point the coaching staff had no choice but to play Heath at tailback. In three games, Heath became the leading rusher for the season, and proved his point to Coach Gran. Regardless of that wrong call, Coach Gran molded some great ones during his Auburn tenure.

Biography

Coach Eddie Gran is the current offensive coordinator for the Cincinnati Bearcats. Gran's twenty-six seasons in the college ranks include stops from coast to coast. It began at his alma mater, Cal Lutheran, where he played four seasons as a wide receiver. He spent fifteen seasons as a running backs coach and special teams coordinator in the SEC, including ten years at Auburn, followed by a stop at Tennessee before coming to Florida State in 2010.

He has also established himself as one of the nation's top recruiters, having spent the better part of two decades recruiting Miami and greater South Florida as his primary territory. He helped the Seminoles attract the nation's No. 1 recruiting class in 2011 and was named one of ESPN.com's Top 25 Recruiters of the Year in 2011.

Gran has a strong record for developing backfield talent. During his fourteen seasons as the assistant to Tommy Tuberville at Ole Miss and Auburn, he sent eight running backs to the NFL, including former Tigers Carnell Williams, Ronnie Brown, Rudi Johnson, Brandon Jacobs, Heath Evans, and Kenny Irons. They were preceded by former Rebels Deuce McCallister and John Avery.

Gran's tenure as a special teams coach included oversight of Auburn kicker John Vaughn, who was the SEC Special Teams Player of the Year in 2006. With his hands-on approach in all facets of special teams play, Gran is widely regarded as one of the most meticulous in tutoring the game's critical "third phase."

Gran has four daughters: Hannah, Dillan, Sydney, and Lucy Grace.

They are deeply involved in the community for a cause that has changed their lives and continues to impact others. The Sydney Gran Foundation is a charity designed to support children's hospitals and other families whose children are facing serious illness. Sydney, the third of the Gran's four daughters, was born with a rare disease called *Holoprosnecephaly*. She passed away just shy of her sixth birthday, in 2005. Additional information is available at www.sydneygranfoundation.org.[1]

---

[1]www.gobearcats.com

The Death of an Angel

By Eddie Gran

My family and I were blessed to have an "Angel" join us on July 1, 2000. All of your children are special, but little did we know just how special Sydney really was.

Sydney was born with a rare brain disease called *Holoprosencephaly* (HPC), in which the brain stops growing early in the pregnancy. We knew something was wrong when she struggled to breath and had a hard time feeding. A trip to Alabama's Children's Hospital in Birmingham changed are lives forever. After the diagnosis of HPC, the doctors' prognosis wasn't very good for Sydney. We were told she would never walk, never talk, have to eat through a feeding tube, and probably wouldn't survive much more than a few weeks.

Needless to say, our world was turned upside down. Twenty-four-hour care for our daughter whom we worried every second might be getting ready to take her last breath. We lost a lot of sleep worrying and everybody was miserable. After a few months of our family trying to make this situation better, Chette Williams, our team chaplain at Auburn University, had a talk with me that changed everything.

He told me and my family to get down on our knees and to give this situation to Christ. He said that He was probably waiting to hear from us, and that all we had to do was surrender through prayer. Our faith was in the wrong place, depending on "man" instead of Christ. We did pray, and we did surrender, and our lives have never been the same since that time.

Yes, there was still pain, and many days that were tough, but we knew Christ was leading our path and He had a plan. We were no longer the captain of the ship; He was. *"Trust in the Lord with all your heart, lean not on your own understanding, think about him in all your ways and He shall direct your path"* (Proverbs 3: 5-6).

We used this verse to help us overcome our adversity during Sydney's tough time. Not only did it help us with her, but it got us through everything we were going through. Now, the losses of a football game, or people saying we were getting fired, didn't consume us any more because we knew where to go to get answers. We made the choice to put our faith in Christ. Our Angel God gave us was changing our family, and we have come to find out she changed many others, too, using her family as her vehicle.

Players and coaches started to see the change in our family. God was preparing us for the day she was leaving, and making us strong so that we could continue her legacy and keep building on our faith. God was so faithful and answered so many prayers. When He took her home, we knew Sydney was whole again, and dancing with the other angels in heaven.

Getting through something like that can only be done with a relationship with our Lord and Savior. Proverbs 3:5-6 is how I try to live my life. Sports, family, failure, it doesn't matter the situation when you have faith and can surrender everything to Him. I am far from perfect, but because of His grace I have received the greatest gift of all for free, eternal salvation.

Our friends, family, Coach Tuberville and the greatest staff I have been around were awesome during this time. Coach was so understanding and compassionate about our situation, and our staff stood in the gap when I had to be gone. Thank God for our in-laws who lived in Auburn, and friends who helped with our little Angel.

I look at things differently now. Football is no longer life and death. I know what that is, and it's not winning or losing games. Football is now a vehicle for me to make a difference, and I try to live my life for Christ and not man.

CHAPTER FIFTEEN

Building Leaders

A leader isn't revealed in times of ease. Rather, true leadership emerges during times of hardship and suffering. When the harvest is plentiful and contentment abounds, almost anyone could be a leader. When the drought is long and the hunger pains intense, a leader finds solutions, encourages vigilance, and rises to meet the challenge regardless of the criticism, the difficulty, or the price to pay. Some are naturally born, some are grown gradually—built by influences significant to their journey. All are unique in style, with results as varied as the individuals themselves. We need different leadership styles because we all respond dissimilarly to diverse tactics.

In athletics, teams go nowhere very quickly without phenomenal leaders. A team without leaders is a team without consistent success. The diversity of leadership styles is just as vast in sport as it is in every other facet of life. There are always a few vocal leaders, teammates willing to stand before the team as a whole, or individuals in a specific unit who verbalize support, demand excellence, prompt emotion, and command accountability. They are energizers and serve as audible reminders of the mission at hand, the effort required, the passionate surge when hope has faded. It's their style, it resonates loudly to many, and it's a vital component of any team.

In my experience, in contrast to the vocal leader was the teammate who led by example. He wasn't the type to articulate frustrations, or express the significance of the moment with his mouth. Instead, he led by his reliability and presence. The trait of this leader was admirable because it was evident without fanfare and pomp, but rather with silent persistence. He led by determination and resolve in the face of dire circumstances. He was the type of teammate you wanted in your corner in a fight, because his actions spoke significantly louder than his words. He didn't want the attention; he wanted the victory, and had the courage and discipline and resolve to lead others toward that end.

Sports places you into an environment to acquire these leadership traits. Some are embedded in your DNA from your parents and your upbringing. Some are a result of the personal experiences encountered under stressful athletic conditions. Some stem from the demeanor and decisiveness of coaches you respected along the way. Some come from adopting current and former teammates' actions and mannerisms. All coalesce to build the leadership scaffolding of the athlete.

We are undoubtedly a sports-obsessed nation. It's something that unites us, young and old, black and white, rich and poor, men and women. We appreciate and place a high value on sports for many different reasons: the athletic prowess we witness; the tactical schemes employed; the loyalties derived from teams representing our towns or cities or universities; the drama associated with watching others compete at a high level, all give us a mixture of pride and marvel and respect. We appreciate the sacrifices made by the players for the entertainment they provide. The players, however, are the true winners, because the leadership characteristics obtained through sports follow them through all of life's endeavors.

The one and only arena that I believe outshines sports in producing leaders is the military. That being said, team sports and the military share several core characteristics. They require selflessness, discipline, communication, unity, repetition, strategy, passion, training, and leaders. The stakes for our military men and women are much greater, but the concepts are very similar. Both provide a leadership backbone to the engaged participant.

Historically, no one is viewed with as much veneration for leadership qualities as the president of the United States. The job brings with it the moniker of "Leader of the Free World." When you consider the many presidents who have served our nation since its inception, a large number of them predictably have military and/or athletic backgrounds. I do not consider that a coincidence. These men likely were gifted with many leadership qualities, but unquestionably many more gained from their experience on battlefields and ball fields alike.

Not every athlete is the leader of a team, nor should he be. We know that in order to have leaders we must have those who are willing to be led. You could have a dynamic player brimming with leadership qualities who is incapable of making a difference because of teammates refusing to buy in to his role. Imagine fighting a war without someone in charge. Imagine riding into battle without solid communications, absolute belief in the soldiers responsible for covering your position, or complete understanding and execution of a masterfully crafted plan of attack. The lack of effective leadership on the battlefield equates to disaster, and possibly death. Thankfully, sports isn't so unkind, nor with consequences so dire; however, the model holds. Walk into a sporting event with a poor plan, a shaky confidence in your teammate, and poor communication, and you'll walk out in defeat.

Some positions in sports force the player into a leadership role simply because of the responsibilities of the position, and the heavy communication required. Quarterbacks directing and exhorting, point guards setting the pace and keeping others involved, and catchers setting the defense and relaying calls from the dugout come to mind. The truth, however, is that any player on a team can rise to become the leader, the teammate everyone can count on to deliver when it matters most. Every person on a team has the opportunity to prove his dedication and desire by demonstrating his tenacity and work ethic when only his teammates are there to witness it. When you have teammates willing to push themselves on a daily basis with an attitude of commitment, they will end up leaders at some point because they are worth following. Vocal leadership is certainly impactful, but vocal leadership from one who also leads by example is exponentially more powerful.

Sports obviously does not transform every athlete into a bonafide leader. Mere participation in athletics does not automatically garner the athlete superior leadership skills, or even guarantee that he will carry over ithe disciplines sport conveyed into his personal life. Sports does, however, surround and impart each and every participant with skills and characteristics they can utilize to lead families, churches, businesses, communities, and all other life undertakings. Not every athlete acquires, or takes advantage, of the skills that surrounds him, but all are exposed to and understand the necessity and impact of that experience. Sports builds leaders.

Alex Lincoln is a case study in overcoming the odds to find success. Overlooked coming out of Murphy High School in Mobile, AL, Alex began his collegiate career at Division III Mississippi College, far away from the bright lights and competition of the Southeastern Conference. Knowing he could contend with the athletes playing at major universities all around him, Alex transferred to Auburn University and became the starting middle linebacker his junior and

senior seasons. But he was far more than just a starter. Alex was the heartbeat of our unit, our leader emotionally as well as strategically, our leading tackler, our leader in and out of the huddle. And he had to earn it. As a walk-on football player, you are required to prove yourself daily to a set of coaches who believe their scholarship player is more talented, and to teammates who expect it as well. With Alex there was no question. Not only would he play, he would excel. He would play through injury and remain accountable to his teammates. He would become our undisputed leader, a warrior with a servant's heart.

Biography

Alex Lincoln joined the EXOS team in 2007 as the general manager of EXOS Gulf Breeze, FL, and would later become vice president of elite business development. During this time, Lincoln and his team have been honored to assist the overall human performance efforts for professional, amateur, and tactical athletes. He's currently responsible for a team of professionals dedicated to serving the United States military and other tactical personnel.

Lincoln graduated from Auburn University, where he was a key member of the Tigers' football program. After a successful collegiate career, he was drafted by the San Francisco 49ers. He spent two seasons with the team before he was forced to retire due to injuries.

After leaving the NFL, Alex founded The Lincoln Group, a company dedicated to providing strength and conditioning services to athletes.

Leadership

By Alex Lincoln

The impact of sports on leadership is a topic often commented on, and far better leaders than I have weighed in on the subject. There are few better training grounds for young leadership than organized sports. It is an imperfect system that presents a model for what the real world is like, unless of course you play in a league where everyone gets a trophy. Athletes must learn to develop work ethic and character in the face of adversity, and a wide variety of personalities and politics. Just as in life, sports can often be unfair.

In my life, the sport of football set the foundation for my leadership philosophy. In the big arena you can't run, you can't hide, and you can't shift blame. Your mistakes are not only out in the open, they are studied over and over. The heat and pressure can be so intense that you aren't always sure you are going to make it. This is where you learn so much about effort and accountability. In today's world, everyone wants to be the leader; yet very few want to take on ownership and accountability in equal measure. In football you either own accountability, or, in most cases, you find yourself off the field. If you can master being accountable to your teammates and coaches, then you have a shot at being a leader and understanding the best form of victory.

All of this, of course, is just the first step toward becoming a strong leader, and I've found that real leadership is being able to serve others in their fight to rise above the heat and pressure. Leadership in the real world is a whole different ballgame, where the players can run, hide, and often shift blame. In this environment, ownership and accountability are truly special. You've got to inspire those who haven't been tested in the big arena. To lead your team, you must seek to understand who they are and discover *why* they are in the game. As a former linebacker, this has been the toughest challenge for me. I've found that tackling someone during a business meeting is frowned upon, so I'm often left to put my early sports experiences aside and take on a different form of pressure. Can you lead those who aren't built like you, and who don't see the world as you do? This is why success in sports is not the total formula for leadership; it's merely a training ground for it. A wise man once suggested that if I thought I was a leader, I should turn around and see if anyone was following me. I've come to learn that a true leader will often be serving and carrying those around him, not just leading the charge towards the goal line.

CHAPTER SIXTEEN

Communication

Is there anything odder than learning to "call" for a fly ball? Those of us with a baseball or softball background remember well the introverted teammate who refused to communicate to the coach's satisfaction. We all thought that the gyrating, demonstrative, take-charge manner the coach enacted was over the top, until the lesson of poor communication burned us. If we were lucky, learning the lesson meant watching a routine fly ball drop between two capable players, frustrating to all. If we were unfortunate, learning the lesson was more agonizing, as the lack of interchange resulted in a terrifying collision. Talking to one another meant not only improving the performance of the team; it also meant protecting each other from the perils of the sport.

My position as safety at Auburn University required me to communicate efficiently and vociferously in order for me to be able to see the field. Communication takes place at every position in football, but the safety position is difficult to match in term s of communicative responsibilities. In fact, I saw the field very early in my career predominately because of my ability to relay defensive alignments and instantaneous adjustments. Being able to successfully recognize offensive formations, and convey the necessary modifications, was far more valuable to our defensive unit than was my athletic ability. I was a good athlete, but a high football IQ was my ticket to success. Having a high football IQ meant very little if I couldn't use that to verbalize effectively to my teammates. Without impeccable communication, a defense is defenseless.

Personally, I am prone to being more passive and introverted, a communicator out of necessity rather than preference. I would rather you do the talking and I do the listening, discerning, and implementing a plan of action. "Owning" a room, board room, a crowd of friends or colleagues, or even my home, has never been a high priority for me. I do not adore the attention, and feel more at ease in the solitude and safety of privacy. Is that wrong? I would say the answer is, yes and no.

Biblically, silence has its high points and is a true gift to those who can employ it. Not a punishing silence, nor a refusal to interact with someone or something based solely out of malice or prejudice, but rather a silence based on fact finding. A silence based on thought preceding articulation. This is a virtue, a true test of character, to be able to tame the tongue with controlled speech. In this way, communicating through intent *listening,* rather than speaking, is honorable.

On the flipside, communicating verbally your belief system, your faith, your hospitality, is how the world defines you and is unavoidable in society. We interact with people every day through the spoken word, and each encounter leaves an impression about the person with whom we've just interacted. As citizens of a country, it is incumbent that our voices be heard when we disagree with intrusive or partial policy, or else we risk losing the freedoms we cherish. Staying silent can result in our being bullied and trampled on. As businessmen, we must interact effectively with our customers, our patients, our bosses, our vendors, our communities, or else we may alienate those who pay our bills. As married couples, we must work hard to be on the same wavelength as our spouses if our marriages are to flourish and grow rather than wither due to disconnect. As Christians, we are called to always be prepared to give an answer to the hope that lies within us. If we can't communicate our faith effectively, we risk the most tragic of results: that those to whom we fail to communicate the Gospel fail to receive life everlasting. Failure to communicate has dire consequences, the latter a tortuous timelessness.

Athletes are well positioned in society to be effective at connecting with those around them. Although not all of us are blessed with the personality type most would expect an excellent communicator to have, athletics teaches the critical importance of interaction and understanding to one's ultimate success. We've all been members of teams that either faltered due to lack of it, or over-achieved due to the careful cultivation of these qualities.

We come from different backgrounds, ethnicities, socio-economic brackets, ingrained predispositions, yet create meaningful and impactful lines of dialogue and deliberation. We are forced to work hand in hand, brother to brother, foster a spirit of cooperation, or else pay with the consequences of defeat and despair. We walk into environments of chaos, conflict, raucous fanaticism, directed towards weakening our resoluteness and piercing the veil of our unity, but unleash a plan of resolve, togetherness, and success based entirely on our ability to communicate extraordinarily within the confines of commotion. Without it, we fail miserably.

Not all communication is verbal, nor does it need to be. In fact, anyone who has entered a stadium in the Southeastern

Conference knows that communication for those of us on the field is rarely verbal. With a crowd of roaring fans, you can't hear yourself scream, let alone your teammate aligned only yards away from you. Hand signals, eye contact, images, instinctive nuances garnered from multiple repetitions with your teammates, all allow for suitable interaction without opening your mouth. We are forced to think outside of the box to make certain our lines of communication are unimpeded, undiscoverable by the competition, and understood by all on its receiving end.

This non-verbal interaction is not exclusive to football. Think of the basketball player who delivers a perfectly timed pass to the rim with only a glance to his teammate who hammers home the dunk. Better yet, think of the catcher who throws behind the runner at first base, picking him off for the out after nonverbal cues to the first baseman. Think of that catcher setting his defense with hand signals, signaling the called pitch to the pitcher, after receiving signals from his manager. Baseball being the quiet sport it is requires probably the most stealth communication structure of all sports. Virtually all strategic communication is unspoken, chatter the lone mechanism to show support and offer pep to your teammates.

No matter the sport, all athletes walk away with a solid foundation and understanding of the importance of communication and its impact on achievement. This easily translates into the professional, personal, and spiritual realm as well. Relationships require work. When neglected, relationships crumble. One thing is certain: you are either growing closer to someone in your relationship, or you are moving further apart. No one is stagnant in this area. The key to growth and progression? Communication. An open dialogue. A strong rapport. Growing your relationship means knowing the person better, and my time spent in athletics helped me to understand the ultimate value of this concept.

When you arrive on campus and start four seasons at quarterback for a program such as Auburn University's, you are more than just a phenomenal athlete. You are indisputably intelligent, undoubtedly ultra-competitive, and certainly anapt communicator. Auburn's all-time passing leader, Stan White, started forty-five consecutive games spanning two coaching staffs, a shift in offensive philosophy, seasons that tallied more losses than victories, and a season that tallied victories only, ending with a perfect 11-0. To play quarterback in the Southeastern Conference requires a special person with undeniable leadership qualities. Chief among these is the ability to effectively communicate. It is not lost on me that Stan, as did my quarterback at Auburn, Ben Leard completed his degree in mass communications. That is what

quarterbacks do. They lead their teams through the messaging they deliver tailored specifically for the individual teammate. Failure to communicate equates to disaster in sport, and in the sport of football it is the quarterback who must be a masterful communicator.

Biography

Stan White was Auburn's starting quarterback from 1990-1993, leading the 1993 team to a perfect 11-0 record as team captain. He still holds the Auburn record for career passing yardage, having started forty-five games in a row. He is a member of the Auburn Team of the Decade for the 1990s, and logged four seasons with the New York Giants before retiring from football and becoming a State Farm Insurance agent in Birmingham. Stan joined the Auburn ISP Sports Network in 1999, and served two years as the television color analyst before moving to radio. At this writing, he will be entering his sixteenth season in the radio booth as color analyst.[1]

---

[1]auburntigers.com

Importance of Communication

By Stan White

Communication, verbal and nonverbal, is essential in most professions. It's the key to success where we turn mental thoughts into physical execution. The same is true on the football field. The "key communicator" on offense is the quarterback. The quarterback not only has to be able to communicate well with the other ten men on the field; he has to exude confidence and precision in the message. Oh, and did I mention, all of this communication has to be relayed at lightning speed.

Let's break it down. When I was playing with the New York Giants, here was one of our play calls: "Ace right trip flip, fullback motion, 'Q' hot Louie, Half 17 quarterback read draw, 'Y' out." That play call tells all ten players on the field at every position what their assignment is for that play. Now, try relaying this play and getting to the line of scrimmage, calling out "hot reads" and everything else involved in about twenty seconds. Not as easy as it appears, is it? Precise communication on the gridiron is essential to success. If one of your teammates doesn't understand or hear your message, then there's a good chance that the play will fail. In a game where we rely on strength, speed, quickness, and overall physical skills, it's the ability to communicate and execute the message that can be the difference between average football teams and championship-caliber football teams.

CHAPTER SEVENTEEN

Character and Integrity

It takes very little time participating in athletics to understand that success depends on much more than merely lining up superior talent. Time and time again in sports, we witness teams with better players lose to players who together make up a superior *team*. We watch as "bigger, faster, stronger" does not guarantee victory as often as "smarter, together, indomitable." Teams with phenomenal leadership and work ethic thrive because the small things are big things to them. Nothing is overlooked or taken for granted. Shortcuts do not exist. This type of attitude breeds success, and ldevelops people abounding with character and integrity.

Barring my parents, no other authority figure in my life had even a fraction of the impact that coaches had on me. Their influence was profound, and affected me far beyond the playing field. One saying I recall even today on a near daily basis is, "Your character is determined by your actions when no one is watching." I heard this statement, or a similar version, constantly, and it did not fall on deaf ears ringing hollow. It produced in me thought and internal investigation in search of who I really was. Not what I presented to the outside world, but who I really was after all the layers were peeled back.

It affected much more than just my consciousness; it affected my schoolwork, my athletic preparation, my spiritual walk, my entire existence. If I couldn't look at myself in the mirror and see honesty and integrity starring back, then what was the point? Who was I kidding? What good would come from deceiving the people in my sphere of influence without a belief in myself at the very core.

Participating in athletics draws out the true character of the individual. Between the physical demands of practice, the rigors of weight training and conditioning, the time management and dedication to study the playbook, the grueling southern humidity, and the relentless prodding by coaches to push you beyond your preconceived notion of your own limitations, you can't fake your way through. If you're a weak individual, you will be broken. If you're a selfish teammate, you will be held accountable by your peers. If you're not willing to work every day to improve your skills, thus improving the team, you will be replaced. You learn humility very quickly in team sports, and that you and you alone are not the only cause of success, but that you and you alone can very well be the cause of failure in any given game.

You learn to respect those in authority, and that there is a time for leading and a time for following. You learn the painful lessons of defeat, dissention, and disappointment, but you gain the valuable insight of the joys of progress, teamwork, unity, completion, victory, accountability, brotherhood. You see first-hand that talk is cheap and results are directly proportional to the effort put forth. You see that your actions, whether selfish or self-sacrificing, affect much more than yourself. Your character is built daily, as each day presents a challenge in some form. How that challenge is met reveals whether that character is built upon a foundation of integrity or one of deceit. Every athlete must face that question daily.

I was lucky enough to have coaches during my transformative high school years who would have willingly lost every game we played if winning had meant sacrificing integrity, honesty, or our character. They did not view athletics as "all about winning," but rather all about molding young minds into what it meant to be men of honor. It wasn't enough to show up and go through the motions daily; it was a requirement to go all out, every day, in a manner worthy of replicating. Athletics did not bring with it an excuse to slack off in other areas of life, but rather an impetus to improve and excel in areas once viewed as weaknesses. Not everyone bought in, nor did all travail result in success or achievement. But we all were given the instruction, tools, and model to become better men. We saw genuine men leading God-centered lives working toward molding our character first, our craft on the field second.

And that is what makes athletes, trained with priorities in order, a prized populace. Little else can prepare men and women for the rigors of life beyond the roof of Mom and Dad. Few activities, organizations, or clubs, can impart as many character-building qualities and scenarios applicable to real world difficulties as can athletics. Not every athlete walks away with integrity as his backbone or is a model citizen, spouse, parent, or person. Not every athlete displays a character worth imitating. But the overwhelming majority would shout in unison that the time spent in their sport was easily the apparatus that built their persona. Sports gave us the opportunity to refine our character in ways nothing else could.

You would never know that Ben Tamburello was one of the most decorated Auburn offensive linemen of all time by interacting with him. He is undoubtedly one of the most humble men I have ever met. Long before Ben became my realtor in Birmingham, helping my family sell and buy homes during perhaps the worst housing crisis this country has endured, I was well aware of Ben's many accomplishments as an Auburn Tiger by virtue of merely flipping through a media guide. His name is littered throughout as a standout lineman who paved the way for some of the greatest running backs college football has ever known.

His sports biography, the Auburn teams he was a part of, the players he went to war with, the championships he won, the victories he helped achieve, are enough to make any former Auburn player envious at the success he enjoyed. But what most impresses me about Ben is this: his athletic achievements pale in comparison to the upstanding person he is in the Birmingham community, the representative he is for the Auburn family, and the passion with which he lives his life. Few people do I walk away from feeling as if they truly have joy in their lives, are truly passionate about others, their family, their faith; but interacting with Ben leaves little doubt. He exudes joy and integrity, and I marvel at that.

Biography

A finalist for both the Outland Trophy and Lombardi Award in 1986, Ben Tamburello was a unanimous All-America selection as a senior at Auburn University, and made *The Football News* All-America squad as a junior in 1985. He anchored an offensive line that led the league in rushing with a 312.5 yards per game average. An All-SEC and Academic All-SEC selection as well, Tamburello blocked for Heisman Trophy winner Bo Jackson and All-America tailback Brent Fullwood during his Auburn career. He established himself as one of the outstanding offensive linemen in the country and, perhaps, in Auburn history.[1]

A member of the Alabama Sports Hall of Fame class of 2010, Ben played five seasons in the National Football League for the Philadelphia Eagles. He has a son and two daughters with his wife, Katy, an Auburn graduate herself. Their oldest child, Ben, is on football scholarship as an offensive lineman at the United States Naval Academy.

[1]www.auburntigers.com

Football's Personal Impact

By Ben Tamburello

I am grateful for my opportunity to have played football for Auburn University and Coach Pat Dye. As a young man trying to make it through his program, I never realized the impact and benefit this time would play in my future, and in every aspect of my life. Some thirty years later, I am reminded daily of relationships forged, experiences both individually and as a team, and lessons learned while on "The Plains."

These include lifelong friendships earned through respect, success and failure in both individual and team struggles, and application of positive and negative outcomes and how to learn from them and "move forward." All of these elements proved to be a training ground for life's eventual, larger and more important struggle and success.

Coach Dye was so effective in using football as preparation for life. His program provided young men with an environment to develop character and integrity through everyday challenges in training, and relating how they can be used later in succeeding in life. One of my favorite quotes from Coach Dye came after the 1983 Sugar Bowl victory over Michigan. "You are going to be in a lot of tough battles next year, year after year ... individual battles with yourself; you won't have teammates with you, but if you'll just look back and think about that January 2 night in New Orleans, gain a little strength from it, then it will help you down the road." Even after such a great season and huge win, Coach spoke of the experience and how we can draw from it later in life. I have thought about that so many times throughout my life!

Establishing goals, preparation, hard work, discipline and structure in your activity, attention to detail are all characteristics learned from football that become second nature. However, some of the greatest lessons come more from within yourself during the experience of struggle and success. Anticipating and overcoming adversity, pushing yourself beyond what you think you can do, expecting and capitalizing on opportunities, and, no matter what the circumstance carrying oneself with poise and confidence. These are learned through the experience of competition, and directly apply in life today.

My oldest child, Ben, has heard me talk about these things his entire life. I believe that, to some extent, they were ingrained in him at an early age. Ben earned a football scholarship at the United States Naval Academy, where he is a junior majoring in political science. My wife, Katy, and I are so proud of Ben, his choice, and his achievements. We know he is tested and challenged daily in so many ways: academically, militarily, in training and education requirements, and in Division I football. I have no doubt that the lessons he is learning are being taught by our country's finest individuals at one of America's finest institutions. I also believe his participation in football will add to his overall experience, and will play a major role in his foundation and in the person he one day becomes.

CHAPTER EIGHTEEN

Overcoming Poverty

The many avenues that exist in life lead to groups of people with vastly differing income levels coexisting in endeavors, sometimes beneficial to both, sometimes divisive and destructive. College athletics is ground zero for just this scenario and provides a unique vantage point for those involved.

The most obvious are the unpaid athletes, deemed amateurs by the authoritative NCAA ruling body, coached by some who are, in many cases, the highest paid public employees in the states in which they reside. In fact, at the time of this writing, thirty-eight states in this country boast football or basketball coaches as the highest paid employees in those states! Rounding out the rest of the states are college presidents or deans working with, and paid by, students who produce no income. The contrasting lifestyles are made most glaringly obvious to the athletes, as they spend so much of their time with the coaches who are paid handsomely. It's the car he has parked in the complex, the watch he wears around his wrist, the pictures of his house or vacation spot in his office. He worked hard for it. He has earned it. As players, we recognized it and applauded it. But it did little to settle the hunger before bedtime, and frustration that resulted from living next to those with excess, but who were prohibited from sharing with those going without.

Even within the team, there were players representing virtually every socioeconomic level. Guys from two-parent homes without a monetary care in the world, rooming with guys who never knew a father and had a mother who worked so many jobs that a sibling had raised them. Some were like me, a middle-class family with working parents, too poor to pay for college, too rich to qualify for a Pell Grant. By comparison, I had it great; although I struggled with lacking the funds for basic necessities everyone in America thought we all had, yet many of us went without even those. Some of my teammates came from absolute poverty, and seeing them make the most of the opportunity of advancement through athletic prowess was all the motivation I needed for me to match their intensity and desire to succeed.

Not all of us shared the same motivation. My drive was internal and personal, a sense of utilizing my gifts to propel me toward a future many around me were not afforded. Giving my all meant moving closer to achieving the reward of recognition and a brighter future. For some teammates, the ambition was more pressure packed and family driven, with socioeconomic difficulties the main motivating factor. This was not only their ticket, but their parents' and siblings' opportunity to escape scarcity. They lived with that burden every day. It broke some. It catapulted others. Raised in the backdrop of Prichard, AL, inner city Miami, or along Alabama's Black Belt, several teammates arrived with nothing, having survived on nothing to get there. An education was important, but it was the instant payoff through football that was the magnet.

Regardless of what you're told, college athletes are not brought in for the education. In fact, education standards must be lowered or flat-out ignored to allow many athletes the opportunity to enroll. Entire academic staffs are devoted to keeping the athlete eligible, not by guidance through daunting curricula, but rather by cherry-picking friendly professors teaching meaningless material. Many athletes are not leaving school with a degree of their choosing, but instead the degree offering the least resistance towards eligibility a staff of athletic department-affiliated academic advisors have hand-selected for him. If they produce ineligible players, they lose their jobs, and the head coach likely loses his job. And this is news to no one. The athlete recognizes the game being played, and devotes his time and energy to his craft on the field above his academic responsibilities. He's being told in no uncertain terms where his priorities should be, and where potential monetary gain is greatest. It will come on the field of play.

For an absurdly small percentage of players, the next level provides for them. They make a career out of professional football. They make it. For most of us, however, the ball does not bounce favorably towards NFL riches. We are forced to fall back on the difficult choices we faced while students. Did we want to coast, or did we want to challenge ourselves? I'm most impressed by those who chose the latter.

The truth of the matter is that college athletics has propelled numerous individuals toward economic success, giving them an advantage over peers in both name recognition and time management, and favorably altering the financial trajectory of generations. We bemoan and wail about perceived slights while on campus (some legitimate, many not) but leave our universities having benefitted greatly from the ultimate marketing campaign any future business person would die for. College athletics has allowed more kids to enter school for the singular purpose of their athletic prowess, yet leave school as a well-marketed employee or entrepreneur. More youngsters and families have seen their fortunes forever altered, rising from the ashes of poverty to the pinnacle of economic success, as a result of their having participated in college athletics.

Do the universities receive a fine deal in this arrangement? Of course they do. They profit handsomely, and I have long held that those athletes should be held to the standard at which they are expected to perform. That is all the extra benefit I would seek. But no one profits from the arrangement more than the athlete. If he takes advantage of all the opportunities that present themselves, if he is serious about more than just being an athlete, then he will far outgain whatever benefit the universities garner. I know I have. I know teammates who came from far less than I did have gained. And we are grateful.

Dameyune Craig could be used as the example in virtually every topic this book discusses. He is an ultra-competitor, and as the senior Auburn quarterback during my true freshman season Dameyune displayed to me an inner motivation and desire to win unlike anything I'd ever seen. He had a passion for Auburn and team and achievement that exuded from every pore of his body. I'll never forget having to stand before the entire football team, coaches and trainers included, and being forced to sing the Auburn Fight Song with my fellow freshman class. Halfway through the song, seeing our lack of spirit and enthusiasm, Dameyune began booing our rendition and forced us to stop. He then ignited

a fire in my heart that will never diminish, as I witnessed him stand in his chair as if he were a conductor, and lead the entire team in an impassioned singing of "War Eagle!" I'll never forget the look on his face, the power in his voice, the emotion he displayed in that moment that showed me what Auburn meant to him. He was our team leader. He was our best weapon. He was our saving grace in many contests. Yet Auburn always remained greater than himself in Dameyune's mind, and rallying behind a leader with that mindset became an easy role for us.

Dameyune hails from an area in Mobile known for producing elite athletic talent, as well as a tremendous amount of poverty and crime. I asked many teammates about their perception of "who had it the worst growing up," and the response was overwhelmingly "the guys from Prichard!" Dameyune is one of those "guys," but he used athletics as a means to a lifetime of freedom from the bondage of poverty in which Prichard held others.

Biography

Former Auburn standout quarterback Dameyune Craig, who helped the Tigers to a 2013 SEC Championship and a BCS Championship berth in 2014, entered his third season in 2015 as Auburn's co-offensive coordinator and wide receivers coach. Prior to returning to Auburn, Craig spent three seasons as the quarterbacks coach and recruiting coordinator at Florida State.

Craig played quarterback at Auburn from 1994-97, where he still holds numerous Auburn passing records, including completions (216) and passing yards (3,227) in a single season, as well as a single-game record for most net yards gained (445 vs. Army in 1996; 75 rush, 370 pass). Craig, who led Auburn to an 18-7 mark in twenty-five career starts, was an exceptional student-athlete on and off the field, earning Academic All-SEC honors as a senior in 1997.

Charged with coordinating FSU's recruiting efforts, Craig's time in that role helped produce the No. 1 and No. 2 recruiting classes in 2011-12, and brought 2013 Heisman Trophy winner Jameis Winston to the Seminoles. Craig was recognized as the 2012 Scout/FoxSportsNet ACC Recruiter of the Year, as well as the Rivals.com ACC Recruiter of the Year. He was named one of the top twenty-five recruiters in the country by Rivals, and one of the top fifty recruiters by 247Sports.

Craig and his wife, Neke, have two sons, Devin Chanse and Drake Christian.[1]

---

[1]www.auburntigers.com

Opportunity through Athletics

By Dameyune Craig

I grew up in Prichard, Alabama, during a time in which crack cocaine decimated my neighborhood. Football provided me an opportunity to better myself by getting a free education. Had it not been for football, I would not have been able to attend college. Most athletes see sports as a means of wealth, and not about getting an education. I didn't; football was a long-term fix for me, a way to change the course of my life and my future. My children will not have to pick up a ball to succeed in life ... because I did! Football has given me generational resources, and for that I am eternally grateful.

CHAPTER NINETEEN

The Loyalty Gene

As an optometrist in private practice in the suburbs of Birmingham, I view as the single most difficult aspect of managing our practice retaining quality employees. Sure, we struggle with government directives and red tape, declining insurance reimbursements, the commercialization of our profession by fly-by-night retailers hoping to make a quick buck, technology utilized without the patient's best interest at heart, and many other nuanced issues impactful to any business. But undoubtedly, hiring and holding on to dedicated employees loyal to the practice is a rare find, and the cause of untold heartburn within the industry. I am certain the field of optometry does not own exclusive rights to this quandary.

Loyalty is incredibly difficult to discover in today's climate of over-sell/under-deliver marketing, the perception of greener grass just beyond our reach, the belief that cheaper price equates to better bargain, or a higher wage is always the superior career path. Loyalty, in my opinion, requires the antithesis of selfishness. It's putting others' interests and immediate needs before your own. Loyalty is hanging in and grinding through difficulties. Loyalty is taking a stand for a cause or person or idea, when the price for doing so is costly, but allegiance trumps perception, opinion, or ridicule. Loyalty is being accountable for your actions, and accountable to those you serve. Loyalty is not blind acceptance, but reliable and faithful commitment.

Athletics represents a unique structure of loyalty on numerous fronts, like little else in life. Developing trust and reliance on your teammate(s) is an obvious component of any successful team, and needs little elaboration. Trusting in your coaches to develop imaginative game plans, creating successful opportunities on game day, is vital. Believing your strength coach's insane method of physical punishment is ultimately beneficial when the time comes to compete against your rival. Certain your fan base will support the effort, even if the effort falls short of victory. Convinced your valleys, whether injuries, playing time, coaching transitions, scholastic difficulties, or losing records, will lead to future unattained heights; success is less meaningful without the backdrop of troubles and trials.

One the most memorable visions I took away from my playing experiences at Auburn University came from the worst season Auburn endured in over fifty years. We had just lost our sixth game in difficult fashion to the Arkansas Razorbacks, 24-21, at home in Jordan Hare Stadium. The prior week our head coach, Terry Bowden, resigned Friday night before Saturday's game with Louisiana Tech. It was a miserable time, a time when allegiance to Auburn on Saturday afternoons must have been a bitter pill to swallow. I'll never forget the feeling I had walking off the field that day, looking at the faces of those fans, standing in their seats, applauding the effort we put forth in defeat, and singing "It's great, to be, an Auburn Tiger!" It was a lesson in devotion and loyalty to me, and it's entrenched into my psyche. Tough times will come; will you stick it out and fight, or will you cower beneath the weight of the challenge, or run from the trial to the path of least resistance?

Loyalty also leaps to the forefront when I consider the walk-on players in any college football program. Here are guys who have made the decision to undertake the complex requirements and demands to become members of their teams, doing so without the reward of a scholarship check, the name recognition, and in most case the opportunity to see meaningful action on Saturday. They devote countless hours to workouts, meetings, and practices, knowing all the while their effort is to see others benefit in competition. They run every sprint, lift every repetition in the weight room, but do not make every trip, see every campus, participate in every game—if any games at all. Yet, no college football program could function without these selfless individuals and their loyalty to the program. And few star players or successful coaches fail to recognize the benefit and achievements obtained through the devotion these unheralded athletes provide.

Loyalty can also be undermined within athletics, and if you participate long enough you will see the converse of allegiance give way to pride, greed, and self-aggrandizement. Unfortunately, the athlete is exposed to both loyalty at its finest, and loyalty sold out to the highest bidder. Sometimes teammates choose the quickest path to the playing field at another school over standing firm and battling for playing time at the school they signed to play for. Many times, coaches ask players to make enormous sacrifices for the betterment of the program, only to watch that coach walk away from his team when lured by a larger payday. Occasionally, a program with a long history of success will see fans alienate and relinquish their role as encouragers and supporters when the season goes south, or results fall short of expectations. Athletes get to see loyalty from many different vantage points. That allows the athlete to gain a unique perspective on allegiance based on real world experiences, where loyalty is passionately on display, and where loyalty is often abandoned for individualism.

Loyalty is under attack in our society at almost every turn. Athletics assists in recognizing the immense value of loyalty, and the unfortunate consequences betrayal and unfaithfulness produce.

Neil Caudle's story is similar to that of several athletes who unfortunately seem to be unduly vulnerable to injuries. As Alabama's top quarterback prospect, and considered one of the nation's elite talents, Neil suffered significant setbacks at numerous intervals during his athletic career. A knee injury struck Neil as a junior at Spain Park High School,

followed by another that ended his senior season occurring on the third play in the second game of the year. A standout baseball player, Neil then tore a ligament in his right thumb that required his third surgery in two years before arriving at Auburn University.

At Auburn, Neil served in a backup role, seeing action in very few meaningful games from his freshman to junior seasons. For a guy recruited from coast to coast, Neil's career had not unfolded as he had envisioned. As a senior, just when it appeared Neil's time to lead Auburn at the quarterback position had arrived, a talented junior college quarterback named Cameron Newton arrived on campus and won the position. Neil could have quit. He could have transferred. He could have wallowed in his own sorrows. Instead, Neil was the model teammate and loyal Auburn man throughout his career. His loyalty was rewarded when he played a key role in the final play of the 2010 BCS National Championship Game, his final play as an Auburn Tiger.

Biography

Ranked as the nation's No. 7 pro-style quarterback, and the No. 8 player in the State of Alabama, by Rivals.com ... Rivals.com Rivals 250 ... Ranked as the No. 163 overall player in the country (No. 18 QB) and No. 44 in the Southeast by Tom Lemming's Prep Football Report ... Ranked No. 122 on ESPN.com's ESPN 150 and as its No. 10 quarterback ... Ranked as the No. 10 quarterback nationally by Scout.com ... Ranked No. 63 on Collegefootballnews.com's CFN Top 150 ... Ranked eighth on CFN's Top 30 quarterbacks ... Ranked No. 15 nationally among quarterbacks by PrepStar ... Ranks 40th on the Mobile Register's Super Southeast 120 list of prospects ... Selected to the EA Sports 2005 Elite 11 ... Rated No. 4 on the Birmingham News Super Senior 2006 ... Named to the Atlanta Journal-Constitution Super Southern 100 ... Injured during the third play of the second game of his senior year, but he accounted for over 250 yards and four touchdowns in a victory over Auburn High in the season opener ... Before his injury, had passed for 224 yards, two touchdowns and one interception on 14-of-26 attempts, and added 51 yards rushing on six attempts ... Missed five games as a junior, but still had 129 completions, 1,634 passing yards and 15 touchdowns, while rushing for 424 yards on 43 carries with five scores ... Named Spain Park's Offensive Back of the Year as a junior. ... Also played baseball at Spain Park, and was named to the Birmingham All-Metro baseball team ... Won the Spain Park Leadership Award his senior year.[1]

Neil currently lives in Birmingham with his wife, Emily, and works as an assistant project manager at Brasfield & Gorrie, LLC.

[1]www.auburntigers.com

Loyalty

by Neil Caudle

My time at Auburn began with hope and expectations of becoming a great quarterback who led his team to championships. Ranked among the top quarterbacks in the country, I had worked out and competed against quarterbacks who would eventually be some of the best players at the college and professional levels. However, my career at Auburn did not go as expected.

After three offensive coordinators, two head coaches, and three lost quarterback battles, I found myself as a fifth-year senior, and third on the quarterback depth chart. At times my football career tested my character, as well as my loyalty to my team, and, more importantly, to my teammates. Spending most of every day with my teammates, and enduring ups and downs with them, we developed loyalty and a sense of brotherhood. Because we had stuck together through tough times, I couldn't fathom not doing everything I could to help them and our team be successful.

Once I realized that I would most likely not see any playing time at quarterback in my final season, I focused my efforts on becoming the best place-kick holder in college football. I know it sounds comical to think about ranking place-kicking holders, but, to me, there were rankings and I was the best. In order for a team to truly be great, everyone must play a role and play it to the best of his ability. My commitment to be the best holder in college football was a microcosm of the approach that our entire team took to the 2010 season. This mind-set played a major role in our success, which led us to the pinnacle of college football, the BCS National Championship.

During the week of preparation for the National Championship, the teams participate in a media day, allowing all national media outlets a chance to interview the players and coaches from each team. A large room was set up to highlight our talented, high-profile players and coaches, with tables and stages everywhere. But occasionally, reporters would break away from the madness and interview a special teams player. I was asked by a local reporter what my dream ending would be to the biggest game of my life. It didn't take long for me to respond that I would like to lead our team on a game-winning drive at quarterback, but if I couldn't do that I would like to hold the game-winning field goal. As it turned out, with seconds left on the clock, tied 19-19, I (number 19), with nineteen seconds on the play clock, held the 19-yard field goal to win the BCS National Championship game.

Although this conclusion to my collegiate football career was far from what I had expected, it confirmed two things for me. First, that my faith in God and his plan for my life and my career, although at times wavering, was completely confirmed. Second, that loyalty and commitment to something bigger than yourself is essential to success.

CHAPTER TWENTY

One at a Time

We are all guilty. As fans, we are all prognosticators as soon as the schedule for our favorite team is released. We rank opponents and strength of schedule months before teams have a single practice under their belts. We've penciled in definitive victories, probable losses, overall records, and possible postseason destinations prior to opening day. We overlook directional opponents with terms like "cupcake" or "gimme" games. We don't respect quality coaching, senior-led or laden teams, or programs on the rise. All most of us see is a name on the schedule, and we make an immediate assumption of the outcome of that matchup based entirely on a name, and the tradition and history that name produces.

In a similar vein, we often overlook the progression of a given athlete, and the brutal journey he took to become the player we see on game day. We love the final product when he out-jumps, out-muscles, out-runs the competition. We marvel at his successes and are frustrated by his defeats. What we rarely consider is the effort put forth out of the spotlight, when a strength and conditioning coach is trying to break him, so that even though a difficult academic course requires a final examination the next day, the strength coach presides over mat drills before the sun rises and expects you to give maximal effort to provide a leadership example for your teammates.

We want to believe that a tutor travels with the player and prepares him for each classroom assignment; that his meals are gourmet and packed with muscle-building nutrients to support an elite athlete in training. We like to think he reflects solely on beating our rival, of honing his skills, of spending any "free time" locked in an office with his position coach poring over film. We want him to be a well-rounded individual, but not as much as we want him to do what is necessary to win football games. That's what he's there to do. Beat our rival. Win championships.

People often ask what was most difficult about playing major college football in the best conference there is. The answer is easy: time management. Prioritizing what was most important, and attacking them one at a time. Athletics taught the lesson of "playing them one at a time." We learned not to look past a "cupcake" opponent, or risk embarrassing ourselves and our fans, and fail to fulfill our aspirations and objectives. That thought process translated well into the classroom by meeting one assignment at a time. A daunting curriculum seemed impossible until broken down one assignment at a time. That was manageable. A grueling two-a-day schedule seemed unendurable until reduced to single practices. Changing your body structure from a an average 205-pound teenager to a 260-pound grown man appeared unreasonable until the daily work produced just that.

As participation in athletics has faded, transitioning into adulthood, marriage, parenting, and working, the lesson holds. A glance at the weekly calendar is harrowing. Work assignments, children's ball games, homework to help with, meetings to attend, church duties to perform, a house to maintain, order to keep—all of it constant, all of it important, all of it demanding. Multiply it by a factor of five in my house with five blessings from God (most of the time!). Athletics, the schedule I was forced to maintain and learn to adapt to, has taught me to take the day in stride, and to prioritize my time to focus on the things that matter most. It has also imparted the wisdom of not overlooking the basics, the small things, the seemingly mundane.

In 2007, Appalachian State opened the season in shocking fashion, blocking a Michigan field goal and stunning the Wolverine faithful 34-32. It sent shock waves through college football. Ironically, it was Appalachian State that we opened the 1999 season against at Jordan-Hare Stadium, winning on a fourth and ten touchdown toss from Ben Leard to Ronney Daniels. We were outplayed from start to finish by a team we should have dominated. Granted, we were not coming off a Rose Bowl appearance like Michigan was; in fact, we were coming off the worst season in over fifty years of Auburn football. Even so, the harsh reality that it took a last-second, come-from-behind, low-percentage play to defeat a team from an inferior college football division was an indictment of our poor preparation for a team we should have run off the field. We had looked beyond the moment toward tougher competition, and were nearly embarrassed to the extreme. Michigan was not so lucky, and the dumbfounded gapes that moment created are forever etched into the psyche of college football fans everywhere. Yet, happen to our team? Never!

Don't underestimate your opponents, the competition, your capacity to sin, your ability to let your guard down. We are all vulnerable to pride, and pride can crush us. We are all guilty of shirking, taking the shortcut, losing focus, and not honing the basics. Some are guilty of overlooking the moment, always caught up in building for the future, and thus missing out on the present. We are guilty of instantaneous judgment without thorough research, knowledge, or understanding. When we get the little things wrong, we fail at the big things. When we are bombarded by the whole rather than content and methodical with the singular portions, we destroy the whole and the whole destroys us—robbing us of joy, satisfaction, success, and life. We can't do everything at once, and we should stop trying. Planning ahead is prudent and necessary, but not at the expense of today. This is an especially difficult lesson for men, me included. Look no further than athletics to observe the principle in action. We all know it. Do we apply it?

Time management is a learned behavior, and is critical to being your best. Time management allows for methodical planning and strategic execution of that plan. In athletics, you build and cultivate a foundation by refusing to allow the basics, the fundamentals, to lapse and leave you with a liability. The greatest schemes devised in football crumble if the fundamentals aren't a given. They are honed daily to allow for successful tomorrows. One day at a time is how champions are made, no matter the endeavor.

Dr. Gregg Carr is a living legend in the city we both share as our hometown, Birmingham. I knew of Gregg's football dominance at Auburn University as a kid—a career that included honors as an All-SEC linebacker three consecutive years, a consensus All-American, the most decorated SEC player his senior season in 1984, and recognition as a Lombardi Award nominee. His stellar play has garnered him entry into the Alabama Sports Hall of Fame, Auburn's Team of the Century, and legendary status within the SEC as he was named to the 2010 "SEC Legend" class.

In addition to knowing of his athletic prominence, I was made aware of Gregg Carr's academic exploits a decade and a half later. Many professors I would have at Auburn University inside the College of Science and Mathematics would recall Gregg Carr as one of their finest students. He attacked academics with the same passion and desire as he did opposing ball carriers, and his intellect was not forgotten by the professors we shared. When my wife developed orthopaedic problems with her wrists, it was Dr. Carr who performed the surgery to relieve the problem. A football legend, an intellectual giant, a successful orthopaedic surgeon, Dr. Gregg Carr has mastered the skill of time management, and has utilized his athletic background as a launching pad towards innumerable successes off the field of play.

Biography

Dr. Gregg Carr is a board certified orthopaedic surgeon in Birmingham, AL. Dr. Carr's passion for orthopaedic medicine has deep roots. As a member of Auburn University football's "Team of the Century," Dr. Carr was recognized as both an Academic All-American and Athletic All-American. After graduating from Auburn University with a degree in engineering, Dr. Carr went on to play inside linebacker for the Pittsburgh Steelers for four seasons.

Dr. Carr's drive to become an orthopaedic specialist began when his professional football merged with his engineering training, creating an enduring interest in the mechanics of human joints. While playing professional football, Dr. Carr completed the requirements for medical school, and in 1994 he received his medical degree from the University of Alabama, School of Medicine. Dr. Carr completed his orthopaedic surgery residency at Greenville Hospital in Greenville, South Carolina, where he also served as chief resident. He was then awarded a fellowship in sports medicine at the American Sports Medicine Institute in Birmingham, where he trained under some of the top sports medicine physicians in the country.

A native of Birmingham, Dr. Carr is a physician who truly understands orthopaedic challenges from all points of view. Surgeon, patient, engineer, parent, football player—Dr. Carr has experienced orthopaedic medicine from all of these angles, and his patients benefit from this exceptionally broad spectrum of insights. His patients, including children and adults, athletes and non-athletes, all receive the same expert care and personal attention.

Dr. Carr and his wife, Juli, have five children: Evans, Jordan, Sara, Grace, and Ann Harrison.[1]

---

[1]www.bhamsos.com

The Lessons of Sport

By Dr. Gregg Carr

Many of the most important lessons in my life were learned as the result of my participation in athletics while at Auburn. These experiences have had, and continue to have, a profound impact on my life. Though I did not know at the time, what I learned about myself, and what the human spirit can endure and accomplish, continues to inspire me.

Today I can appreciate the good fortune I had of being a member of Coach Dye's first football team at Auburn during the spring of 1981. However, at the time, I did not feel so fortunate. For those too young to know or too old to remember, Coach Dye inherited a football program that was average at best, and probably not much better than a great high school football team. He took a football team submerged in a quagmire of mediocrity, without direction and focus, and gave the team a purpose. He challenged a group of young men, many of whom didn't believe in themselves, and convinced them to believe in him and his system, and in doing so left an indelible impression on many of those players, including myself. Coach often said that, when you get knocked down, the only reasonable option is to get back up and try harder. He molded a group of individuals too stubborn to quit into a football team that would ultimately compete with the best teams in the country, and that would have a legitimate shot at winning the national championship just two years later.

Coach Dye's secret to success was simple. First and foremost, he believed in hard work and preparation. During his first spring football practices, he focused on the fundamentals of football. Practices consisted of tackling and blocking, over and over; nothing fancy, just the monotonous fundamentals for what seemed like months, but which, in reality, was fewer than thirty days. He accepted no excuses. Many of my teammates quit. All of us thought about quitting. I remember Coach Dye telling us during one of our meetings that if you quit you would always be known as a "quitter." To me, the only thing worse than the treatment we endured on the football practice fields would have been being labeled a quitter.

Coach Dye always seemed to know the right buttons to push. We finished that first spring football practice with far fewer football players than we began with one month earlier. Fortunately, this team made up for what was lacking in talent with heart and determination and resolve. At the completion of that first spring football training, those few players who fought the fight, and survived physical and emotional battles on and off the field, had developed an incredible willpower and commitment to excellence. No task or challenge seemed unreachable or beyond our capability. Coach Dye's methodical and unrelenting demands, and the expectations he placed on his players, had fostered a mental toughness that would prove to be key to his, and our, success. Coach Dye's goals became our goals, and we became believers in his system. If a game was close in the waning minutes, we felt we deserved to be the victor because we believed we worked harder and prepared more thoroughly than any other team in the country. Whether that was true was irrelevant. We as a team believed this, and that mindset was hard for our opponents to overcome.

As a result of my experiences at Auburn, I feel athletics teaches athletes far more about *life* than it does about sports. On a daily basis, I utilize the lessons gained from competitive sports participation. Coach Dye told us many times that he was not simply preparing us for football games, but for life. It can be hard for a nineteen-year-old kid to understand the perspective of an individual older and much wiser, but as I, too, grow older, Coach Dye's lessons become much clearer and resonate much louder with me.

I am often asked what lessons I learned from Coach Dye. What was the secret to Coach Dye's success? As I mentioned earlier, I think the secret to his success was his belief in hard work and emphasis on setting goals. Coach Dye made it sound so simple. In theory, it is simple, but in reality it proves to be very difficult.

Accomplishing goals often requires hard work. Hard work requires commitment. It is difficult to be committed to a project in which you don't have absolute faith. Without commitment and discipline, it is easy to become distracted and lose focus. One must have a strong desire to make the sacrifices often necessary to accomplish our goals. This is much easier said than done. Coach Dye realized that each individual had certain strengths and weaknesses, and that it was important to utilize our strengths to overcompensate for our weaknesses. He provided us with an algorithm, or a framework, for pursuing and accomplishing our goals, and, more importantly, the confidence to do so again.

Having goals is essential to success. Possessing drive, determination, and other intangibles, are imperative to achieving tangible goals. Very few people succeed in life without encountering many failures along the way. These failures build character, and require the kind of strong mental attitude and resolve that make the ultimate successes all the more rewarding. In other words, it is not only the fulfillment of a goal that builds character, but also the pitfalls one experiences during the journey. And what a journey it has been since those character-building sessions on the practice football fields at Auburn more than thirty years ago. I'm sure Coach would be happy to know that, when I get knocked down, I'm still getting back up.

CHAPTER TWENTY-ONE

Value of Varied Abilities

Two positions in football at the collegiate and professional level I always felt a sense of bitterness toward were kickers and quarterbacks. At almost every practice, the quarterbacks were protected from being hit with unlike-colored jerseys, and with coaches exhorting, "Stay off my quarterback!" Those players were able to walk into any practice, perhaps overwhelmed by the mental aspects of their position, but free from worry with regard to the physical punishment a practice entailed for the rest of us. It gave me the feeling that I was expendable, while the third team QB was worth protecting at all costs.

The kickers were even worse. They practiced by themselves, without a coach from the staff even there to prompt any sort of emotional angst. They had their own coach with them, usually some soccer guru, since the regular staff had no idea how to coach a kicker. They, too, were protected from live contact, so the threat of bodily harm was a non-issue each and every day. There were instances in my career when practice was abnormally brutal and I happened to see the kickers and snappers sipping water on their field in between plays of an impromptu two-hand-touch football game. It annoyed me like few things could.

During the week of practice, those two positions were the object of my envy. I resented my practices being both mentally and physically exhausting while, from my vantage point, theirs was a cakewalk. I resented it all the way until game day, when the field goal kicker was asked to kick a game-winner against a bitter rival in miserable conditions—cold from being a spectator for most of the game. I resented it all the way until I saw the quarterback meeting with the offensive coordinator prior to the game, as they walked through all of the detailed responsibilities that would be his during the game, the enormity of the responsibility to put his offense in a good position with each play call, and the pressure and blame that came with that positon. Then I was grateful for my position, and the fact I wasn't a kicker or a quarterback. I respected each immensely, and recognized that our team loses games when these two positions performed poorly. I could play terribly and we could still win by several touchdowns. They did not have that luxury.

Similarly, my judgment of their lack of physical prowess was misplaced. If you have ever tried to kick a football through the uprights, you know it is far more difficult than it looks. Constantly swinging that leg to fine tune a kicker's precision must be delicately balanced against protecting the kicker's leg from fatigue and injury. The stretching, practice, and therapy that goes into being a kicker is exceedingly complex. The symbiotic relationship he, the snapper, and the holder must share is uncanny, as this trio must act flawlessly as one organism. In many instances, the kicker gets blamed for the holder's ball placement error, or the snapper's poor delivery that fatally alters the timing. The fans, coaches, and teammates expect perfection at every opportunity, yet yawn when it is delivered well, and fume when it is not. Their position is a thankless craft most times, one I'm glad I never had to endure as a player, and one I wouldn't wish on my children.

Just like the kicker, the quarterback walks a very fine line between strengthening his arm with multiple throws versus injuring or fatiguing his arm by overthrowing. He has the enormous disadvantage of taking multiple hits during a game without the bodily adaptation that repetition affords. Therefore, he deals with postgame soreness in a way different from that of his teammates. The quarterback receives far too much credit when his team is victorious, and far too much blame when his team is beaten. He must receive the play call, communicate the play to his offense, initiate any pre-snap movement to confuse the defense, read the defensive alignment, change the play called to a better one if the defensive alignment warrants, receive the snap, read a moving defense, and find the open the receiver. All of this, and he has not even thrown the pass, which is how he is ultimately judged. He must then deliver a precisely thrown pass while ignoring men twice his size closing in on him to do bodily harm. No, thanks! I'll take my safety slot, and gladly give him the thrill of being the quarterback, with all the negatives attached.

It is easy to overvalue our own roles and abilities on a team, an organization, a family, a church, yet undervalue the roles or talents our peers perform. What appears easy from a distance can muster newfound respect when attempted by the onlooker. The service one person gives may appear trite, until you've had the need for that very service in your own life. Team sports doesn't always get it perfect, but it does teach one to value and respect the roles and abilities of others. This is an incredibly powerful and vitally important character trait to have, as it imparts humility and a healthy respect for even the most mundane tasks people contribute to our society.

> *As the Apostle Paul teaches in Romans 12:4-9: "Just as our bodies have many parts and each part has a special function, so it is with Christ's body. We are many parts of one body, and we all belong to each other. In his grace, God has given us different gifts for doing certain things well. So if God has given you the ability to prophesy, speak out with as much faith as God has given you. If your gift is serving others, serve them well. If you are a teacher, teach well. If your gift is to encourage others, be encouraging. If it is giving, give generously. If God has given you leadership ability, take the responsibility seriously. And if you have a gift for showing kindness to others, do it gladly."*

We do not all have the same talents, gifts, or abilities, and thank God for that. If we all were alike, what a perfectly boring world we would live in. If everyone were like me, we would have no functioning automobiles or machines of any kind, and no concept of computer software. If everyone were like my wife, we would have no maps and no fried foods. Our differences in society scare us, but also make us great. Place a high value on the abilities of others, and be grateful for our distinctions.

Cody Parkey was the ultimate special teams weapon, a coach's dream, during his Auburn career from 2010-2013. Handling both kickoff and field goal duties with stunning power and remarkable accuracy, the Auburn kicking game flourished with Cody at the helm. After signing a free agent contract with the Indianapolis Colts, and subsequently being traded prior to opening day, Cody landed in Philadelphia and won the kicking job—a steep uphill battle for rookie free agents. All Cody did in his first season as an Eagle was break the NFL's long-standing rookie scoring record, as well as earn a trip to the Pro Bowl. His talent is unique, and

was recognized by his peers as one of the best in the game. But what about his teammates? What about his coaching staff? What about the fans, the expectations placed on a kicker, the no-win situation kickers find themselves in—their successful performance expected as almost automatic, and looked upon as abject failures and liabilities when the execution of what looks so simple goes awry? Kickers train differently, are coached differently, practice differently, prepare mentally differently. They are integral members of a team, potentially holding enormous power and sway over the outcome of a game and over the success of a team, while performing a job no one else on that team can come close to accomplishing. They are kings when they connect at the buzzer, goats when the uprights are not split and the game is lost. Their talents are more specialized, and wholly unlike, those of their teammates, which makes kickers a valuable commodity in football. They are the "foot" in football. But are they respected?

Biography

Signing with the Auburn Tigers out of Jupiter, FL, in 2010, Cody Parkey's high school honors included being named the No. 1-ranked kicker by ESPN.com/Scouts Inc. ... ranked by Rivals.com as the No. 1 most accurate kicker, and the No. 6 kicker overall ... 2010 Under Armour All-American game ... named to the PrepStar All-America team. His Auburn career consisted of such honors as being first in the nation with 69 touchbacks his senior season ... had his SEC long string of 90 consecutive PAT kicks made (seventh nationally) snapped by a blocked kick at Tennessee ... ranks in top 5 in all Auburn kicking categories ... 142 of 248 career kickoffs were touchbacks (.573) ... career long

52-yard field goal in SEC Championship Game vs. Missouri, a title game record ... 22-yard make, 33-yard miss vs. Florida State in BCS title game ... Lou Groza Award watch list ... preseason second team All-SEC (SEC coaches, SEC media, Phil Steele, Athlon) ... Phil Steele mid-season 2nd-team All-SEC ... December, 2013, graduate in communication ... Senior Bowl most outstanding specialist ... SEC Academic Honor Roll.[1]

---

[1]www.auburntigers.com

Respecting the Kicker

By Cody Parkey

During my time at Auburn, and as a Philadelphia Eagle, I believe I earned, and have always had, the respect of all my teammates. The respect earned is more now than ever, because the guys realize how much pressure you're under as a kicker. I have gotten nothing but love from the fans as well, saying how much they appreciate me for representing them on and off the field in a positive way. The value of a kicker is overlooked by some, but from my experiences at the highest level in football, the players, fans, and coaches realize how important and vital you are to the team. They respect what you do just as much as they do everyone else on the team.

CHAPTER TWENTY-TWO

Calculated Risks

Critics have surfaced in recent years concerned about head injuries suffered in football, and whether the sport is a health hazard for those participating. Landmark concussion lawsuits at the sport's highest level, the National Football League, have opened eyes and piqued the curiosity of seemingly everyone—from neurologists, government bodies, plaintiff attorneys, coaches, and the athletes themselves. As a former football player having the opportunity to compete at every level of the sport, the single most frequent question I receive is, "Knowing the risks involved, would you let your kids play football?" It's a fair question with an easy answer—with a caveat.

If my children expressed a desire to play football, I would certainly not stand in the way. I would encourage participation, and be thankful that the yearning to take part in a game that teaches, molds, and grows character unlike anything else I've experienced in life has taken root in them. I owe a great deal to the sport, and to the coaches who invested time and energy into my life, and I would be joyous if my children could share in that experience. But here's the stipulation: I would not allow my boys to play football until they have reached the age when they are coached by professionals paid to coach them.

The only way I would budge on that requirement would be if I myself were the coach, or someone I was certain taught proper fundamentals and technique was at the helm. Which begs the question: If football, and the coaches who came with the sport, were such a powerful, influential force in my life at a very young age, setting the course for the path I would take, why would I limit the exposure of my own kids at a young age? Are the dangers not worth the benefits of the ultimate team sport? Do the risks outweigh the rewards? Yes, and no.

Yes, undoing poor habits taught by well-meaning but technically uninformed fathers is problematic for me. But it's the repetitive impact drills to a developing young child I would seek to avoid, especially the way they are taught and executed by dads rushing to practice after work. And even with a technically superior, experienced, well-intentioned and trained coach, I would hesitate to send my elementary-aged boys onto the practice field for full contact football. At that age, yes, the risks outweigh the rewards for me, because non-contact football could effectively allow for many of the positive attributes football bestows without the inherent risk of long-term brain injury. It also would help prevent burn-out as the child approaches the middle and high school years, when he can most enjoy and appreciate the impact football can have on his life.

As the kid enters adolescence, he can more effectively become involved in a sport because he chooses to rather than because his parents forced him. The kid is more likely to be coached by someone paid and trained to do so and would, therefore, be free from bad techniques that are outdated or improper and is at a stage to be properly molded.

Isn't head injury still a risk, even if he has matured and entered into the puberty stage of life? It absolutely is, and will forever be a risk at any level of football. But now, in my opinion, the reward far exceeds the danger. We have minimized the risks as much as possible through avoidance of years of contact, years of bad habit formation, years of exertion that accumulate towards burn-out. But at this point, a life without football for the youth who wants to participate is a life deprived. Go play—have fun—and build a lifetime of positive character traits that will be entrenched within your persona.

The truth is, head injuries are possible in any sport. We can find fault across the entire athletic landscape. We could legislate away sport after sport in the name of safety, and pat ourselves on the back for saving generations of kids by keeping them out of harm's way. We could make tennis players wear eye protection, gymnasts wear pads and braces, baseball players wear face shields, and better protect every athlete in competition. We do not, because the risk is low and the value the sport has in the life of the competitor is high. If studies produce results showing that brain injury is likely from football participation, I would still advocate for the continuation of the sport and the participation of my boys, because I recognize what a vital role the sport played in who I am today, and would trade years of my life for the powerful attributes gained from football.

I certainly sympathize with athletes who become debilitated because of football. I obviously hope and pray that my life, or the lives of my loved ones, are never impacted negatively from athletic-related play or injuries. I am certain that every high school and college teammate I had would go back and play again, aware of the medical risks we now know about. We'd do it because we loved the exhilaration and challenge of competition, teamwork, and seeing goals and dreams realized after sacrificing so very much. A sport without sacrifice, one that comes easily, fulfills only marginally and teaches the athlete very little about himself. In football, you lay it all on the line every single day, and the experiences, lessons, and traits instilled provide a lifetime of social, spiritual, and personal wealth.

The combination of Coach Jack Crowe's football coaching experience, and his extensive background in sports safety, makehim uniquely qualified to further the conversation on player safety in the sport of football.

Professional Biography

In addition to his accomplished college football coaching career spanning more than forty years, Coach Jack Crowe is the past Executive Director of the American Sports Medicine Institute (ASMI) where he worked with Dr. James Andrews in education and sports injury prevention. He is the most experienced and qualified professional to address issues that cross over the two domains of sports medicine and sports participation.

Crowe has long had a pioneering interest in the education of parents and coaches. He has testified in the Kentucky State Legislature on "best safety practices" in coaching. His academic background in the basic human sciences, and as an instructor in kinesiology and the care and prevention of injuries, gives him the credentials to represent himself as a coach, an educator, and as a sports medicine professional.

That interest led to his involvement with medical providers and continuing education providers in initiating programs that address the parent and the coach as part of the sports medicine continuum. His professional services are focused on sports education. With a master's degree in counseling, Crowe also addresses the social dynamic of sports trends as they relate to the total sports experience for all youth.

He is the president of Strategic Solutions, LLC, which is the personal services and consulting company he formed in 1990. His focus is now on providing a strategic solution to all the stakeholders involved in youth sports. He believes that to deter what is becoming a public health problem, vested parties should be challenged to join a sports injury coalition with the goal of banding together to enable change.[1]

[1]www.coachsafely.com

Player Safety

By Jack Crowe

Having participated, observed, and been an influence on community football for my entire life, today I have a compelling allegiance to the game, and I have major concerns about the future of community football. My life experiences have validated for me the fact that youth football is a vital part of the social fiber in every community in this country. And my utmost respect is for all community sports coaches, because they are their communities' residing authorities in the sports they coach, as well as the guardians of the public trust in the values of sports.

Since the 1960s, as an athlete, a coach (forty years) and a parent, I have seen athletes and their parents change in as many ways as our American society has changed. In those last fifty-plus years and continuing into today, the generations of men who coach football to our country's youth are also being transformed as part of our changing society. I feel that the transformation of community football coaching has been socially chaotic, rather than value based. An affecting element of such change is that community sports has escalated into a multi-billion dollar business. For young people, ages six to nineteen, who play the games, community sports in the United States has long offered social value as a character-building experience. The promise of that experience began with sport's integration into American society under the leadership of President Theodore Roosevelt at the turn of the twentieth century. Community sports in America have been evolving for the hundred-plus years since then.

Participating in youth football, when coached properly, provides the benefit of developing boys into the most self-confident, resourceful, and socially responsible adults that their innate traits will allow of them. The community youth sports experience has also evolved more recently into a critical, but unregulated, instrument of our country's public health guidelines, by providing an early pattern of activity for children as a foundation for a lifelong active and healthy lifestyle. But the last six decades of social changes have also created a social problem, with sports fulfilling its social mission. Recent information, such as the "sports and society" study developed by the Aspen Institute, strongly suggests that this unregulated public health instrument, as well as the overarching social value promises of community sports, is failing because of the increasing public dissatisfaction and high "drop-out" rate of the youngest sports participants. The result of this failure of American youth sports to fulfil its social mission is that our society is becoming less healthy and less productive.

Thought leaders across multiple public domains have come to associate two of the primary reasons for the decline in youth sports' social value, and in the declining youth participation in sport: one, the lack of professionalism in community sports coaching; and two, the increasing rate of injury to youth sports participants. Injury risks, which once were acknowledged as an inherent part of sports, are today being seen as mostly preventable. One thought trend that puts the highest priority on coaching education as a remedy reasons that the growing lack of professionalism in youth sports coaching is a partial cause for the increasing rate of injuries.

The cost of these preventable injuries (in all sports) to our children's sports dreams and experience—as well as the cost to the nations' declining public health as a result of the youth sports "drop-outs." presumed inactive lifestyles consequences—is immeasurable. The cost also extends to Medicaid and private pay insurers, and to liability carriers. The combined health-care cost for treatment of youth injuries in sports is approximately 2.5 billion dollars a year. Related later health consequences can account for another three billion dollars a year. Emergency room visits alone are costing one billion dollars a year. States can enact policies in interscholastic and recreational sports that would mitigate the current escalating epidemic of youth sports injuries and that would at the same time add professional standing to community coaches, by requiring (as the public health intervention) coaching education in youth sports injury prevention. Evidence that an educational intervention reduces health-care and insurance costs and affords sports injury immunity for state sponsoring organizations, would be a plausible incentive for state governments to mandate new policies.

Football is America's favorite sport. It is also the most physical sport, and it requires more contact than other sports. But it does not have the highest incidence of injury, and actually it is fourth in that category. Football, however, is the most highly visible tip of the iceberg. Coaches in community football are under more scrutiny than those in any other sport because of the negatives that have trickled down from the NFL and NCAA Football class-action plaintiff lawsuits filed by former players. Most coaches are guilty to some degree of letting the motivation to win circumvent their judgment to prevent injuries. A working knowledge of the science of sport is the most relevant deficiency in the coach's judgment to prevent injuries. Caregivers who volunteer to support community coaches are making a great effort filling the knowledge gap when they are present. The behavioral intervention that would mitigate injuries begins with coaches learning the risk factors and the identification of early signs of injury; that requires administrative and the caregiver's support. Learning the science of performance and injury prevention as integrated and equal concepts within the framework of coaching would define a coach as a professional. Community football may need that intervention to survive.

Current trends in public opinion are responding to the narrative coming from national news and sports media, which are advocating for changing the sports culture, and for revolutionizing sports coaching. The domains of coaching and sports liability are on a collision course that could result in changing the dynamics of the coach's role in sports. The authority of the coach to direct the athlete in the training, skill development, and in the competition of the sport, will be greatly compromised if he cannot *coach safely* (also the name of his organization, Coach Safely). The latitude that coaches now have to develop the performance of the athlete will become restricted by limitations on coaching methods. At that point, enforcement will become a major oversight challenge for administrators. Coaches are seen today as community leaders whom parents trust will teach their children the skills and values that sports promises, but the most recent trends indicate that parents are becoming less trusting. And *parental fear of injury* is suggested by thought leaders as another reason why participation in youth sports is declining.

A recent, highly publicized sports injury incident (the 2014 Michigan vs. Minnesota football game) became a policy-defining event directed at the public's right to know who has the vested responsibility and authority for the well-being of the athlete. "Which leader had failed in his responsibility?" After the national public uproar, the athletic director at the University of Michigan made a public statement, following a sports concussion/return to play controversy, that the responsibility for the well-being of the athlete was, first the coach, then the sports administrator. According to that statement, the top sports medical professionals who were on the University of Michigan's sidelines at the time presumably lacked the authority or influence.

Obviously, no sports professional continuum of care and prevention existed on the University of Michigan sideline. The corresponding highly publicized statement also, in effect, pointed the liability away from medical and administrative personnel and put it on the coach. The appropriate and valid point made in the Michigan athletics director's public statement was that the coach is the competitive leader. The coach is not the medical leader or the administrative leader, but the domain of competition is the coach's domain, and that includes all the intangible aspects of sports. *The dilemma for all youth football in this country is that, even as the recognized leader in teaching the values of sport, the football coach in today's environment of injury fears and social judgments is beginning to lose the trust of parents and public thought leaders.*

It is important to consider this and other controversial public sports injury events at the national level in the context of its effect on sports in local communities. Public injury events at the professional and collegiate levels of sport trickle down to community sports, affecting attitudes and practices, and because of the media thethat effect is expeditious and widespread. Unlike professional and collegiate athletes, youth athletes live at home, and their parents have the primary responsibility for their well-being. In communities, it is the parents who should provide the public oversight of the community school and recreation sports programs. Unfortunately, parents today in general are assuming too much from the traditions of sports. And when parents have concerns, most often they are uneasy expressing them to the coach. The lack of effective administrative best practices (including communicating with parents), and the educational gap for coaches in sports science in the majority of communities, has not as yet become fully apparent to parents. These are the two major reasons why the risks are greater today, especially to the younger athletes, and probably even more so to female than male athletes. Participants at every level have parents and families who are responsible for their children's well-being. And it is parents that are the core constituency of the public trust in community sports.

Today's looming crisis over the coach's increased authority, and the potential consequences, will intensify because the risks are escalating for today's sports coaches, in part because of the declining "physical literacy" of todays' youth athletes. They are less capable of accepting the physical demands of training that uses antiquated coaching methods from a generation ago. Air conditioning, video games, poor nutrition, and a lack of "free play" opportunities, is becoming more and more the lifestyle that predisposes youth today to a higher risk of injury in sport. And compounding the "physical literacy" dynamic is the emergence of youth "professionalism." Parents have become a primary instigator of over-training young children for the goal of recognition, scholarships, and professional careers. This is resulting in parental pressure on coaches being a significantly greater dynamic in community sports than in previous generations, a problem that is requiring more effective sports administration.

The public today does customarily trust that the coach has some training, and that he or she understands the risks and causes of preventable injuries. However, without a professional standard based on an education process for coaches, and without administrative oversight, such public trust is misguided. Public events have and will continue to happen that undermine the public trust. I was involved in such a public event that started in August 2009, when a tenth grade football player died after collapsing on the practice field from the effects of several consecutive days of heat exposure. It happened at Pleasant Ridge High School in Louisville, Kentucky. The parents of the deceased player charged the Pleasant Ridge head football coach with wrongful death, and it went to trial. During the period before the trial, the Kentucky State Legislature held a legislative hearing before the Joint Committee on Education. I was the coach asked to testify. The questions to me from the members of the committee all revolved around whether the coach who had been charged violated professional standards, and thus created a legal liability. I had no doubt about the coach's motives and intents, and I did not feel that he had violated any standard of "coaching tradition," but my message to the legislators was succinct and calculated. I responded,"There is no standard of coaching that could have prevented this player's death."

"Standard of coaching" is not an accurate term for an assessment of coaching methods. "Coaching trade practices" is a more accurate description of a coach's training (which is different from education). Actually, all heat-related death is preventable where there are integrated *prevention concepts* in place. The coach's educational background was never addressed. And currently, there is no standard that requires the coach to have the knowledge that would have prevented the athlete from dying. The coach had no standard to hold him responsible. If the Michigan athletics director's policy statement had been part of the public record, the lack of a "plausible denial of knowledge" may have affected the outcome of the trial. The coach was found innocent of the charges. The stepfather later said, about charging the coach, that he knew that circumstances would prevail, but he wanted to focus public attention on the case in order to prevent a future occurrence.

The media obviously has a strong influence on the public trust, and focuses its coverage on failures of sports leadership, especially when it carries liability, as we have seen in the legal actions against school systems, the entities that govern sports, and against providers for sports. The NFL and NCAA are both defendants that have settled with enormous paid damages. At the national, state, and community levels, the media message is contributing to the erosion of public trust. The Aspen Institute (a high-profile media source in public policy) will add to the public message.

All of this public messaging alert sports organizations to the fact that they are liable for the actions of their coaching assignees, and to the legal claims that place them in the position of being defendants. The injuries obviously are resulting from sports activity at practices, or in games that are being directed by the assigned coaches. The coaches are the gatekeepers of prevention. When coaches lack the knowledge, awareness, or motive to make decisions that prevent injuries, the liability inures to the organization that assigned the coach. Plaintiff claims are made against the organization that is financially answerable. The public is realizing that it is the coach who determines the activity regimen, and who has the authority over the participation that exposes athletes to risk. With all that the media foreseeably will report, it is predictable that parents' in the coaching profession will continue to have an incremental reversal because of plaintiff claims, and with ongoing media coverage will come an escalating indictment of the current culture of all sports, but targeted especially at football.

CHAPTER TWENTY-THREE

Seizing the Opportunity

Team sports offer unique opportunities for an athlete to demonstrate his individual impact on the results of a contest. Though great players often find avenues to succeed, on occasion their athletic prowess is matched or surpassed by a superior player, by a strategy devised by an opposing coach, by such unforeseen circumstances as injuries or illnesses that level the playing field, by being unable to overcome the deficiencies of his teammates, or by just flat-out performing poorly in any given game.

All team sports have competition for positions. Nothing is given at the highest levels of team sports. Fierce battles are waged for playing time, for the opportunity to represent a town, a city, a university, a franchise in sports of all types, in leagues and divisions, and in all age groups. When your opportunity arises, the response must be to meet or surpass the expectations of your coaches and your teammates, and marshall your inner drive to rise to the occasion, and perform admirably. In short, you must seize that opportunity.

Courtney Rose played safety at Auburn during my entire career there. He redshirted the year before I arrived on campus, a prolific high school running back from Hazlewood High in Town Creek, AL, and converted to safety at Auburn by Coach Bill Oliver. He wore number 30; I was number 31, so our lockers were right next to one another for four years. He was a terrific teammate, a bright engineering major, a lighthearted guy easy to talk to and as laid back as anyone you'd ever meet. Courtney was an all-around good guy.

As a true freshman, I battled Courtney and several other upperclassmen to win the safety position. By week two, our home SEC opener versus Ole Miss, I was the starter. I retained my starting position for the duration of our careers. Occasionally, we would play side by side a series or two throughout our careers, but predominantly Courtney was relegated to backing me up. He never complained. He never spoke ill to me. He never quit working or took it easy. He never made me feel guilty, or gave me the impression he was hurt by his lack of playing time at my expense. He encouraged me throughout our Auburn stint.

The summer prior to our senior season, I spent more time in doctors' offices searching for a diagnosis for the muscle cramping I was suddenly afflicted with than I devoted to conditioning and lifting weights. By the time fall camp began, I was in no condition to begin practice, so Courtney took nearly all the repetitions. My absence created an opportunity for Courtney to establish a comfort level with the first team, and to develop chemistry with the guys who line up on Saturdays.

In the first game of the season we basically split repetitions. Since we were both seniors, our defensive coordinator left it up to us to substitute in and out for one another whenever we saw fit. Courtney and I decided we would try to rotate every series. In truth, I felt as though Courtney deserved more playing time than I did, considering the work he had put in during my absenteeism. He had endured all the two-a-days, the heat, the conditioning, the mental and physical grind, while I struggled with routine daily activities. On the other hand, I believe Courtney respected me enough as a player and friend to allow me entry back into the playing rotation despite my condition, due to the amount of football I had played and the heart I always demonstrated. In truth, Courtney probably felt badly for my physical and mental state as our last season had arrived.

Week two had us traveling to Oxford to play a primetime clash with a resurgent Ole Miss squad, televised nationally on ESPN as Coach Tommy Tuberville returned to Ole Miss for the first time since departing for Auburn. Ole Miss was ranked in the top twenty and the favorite to win on a night so humid that breathing felt as though it was being done through a soaked wash rag. I started the game. Ole Miss drove eighty yards in twelve plays, connecting on an eleven-yard touchdown pass. And that was it for me. I felt as if I had been swimming for hours in mud. The heat, combined with my rudimentary conditioning, forced me to the locker room for IV fluids and Vitamin B12 shots. I was toast, and there would be no substituting by me on this night; the position belonged to Courtney for the duration. It was his time to seize the moment.

Courtney played the game of his career in an environment where superlatives were needed to walk out a winner. He tallied seven tackles, which was second on the team, including one tackle for a loss. In the second quarter, leading 14-7, Courtney timed a safety blitz to perfection, dropping the Ole Miss quarterback for an eleven-yard sack on third down ending that drive. And with us leading by one point midway through the final quarter, with Ole Miss driving for the go-ahead score, Courtney intercepted the Ole Miss quarterback on a third and nine pass attempt, which led to a final Auburn touchdown that iced the game. He was named SEC Defensive Player of the Week, an honor well deserved. I started forty of the forty-seven games I played in at Auburn and was never recognized as SEC Defensive Player of the Week. He didn't just seize the opportunity; he exceled to the extreme. He was prepared for the moment, making critical plays that thrust Auburn to victory.

The next week, a home tilt against LSU, ushered in a cold front that allowed me a reprieve to a degree. We rotated every series all the way to the Citrus Bowl on New Year's Day. We finished that season with virtually identical stats, and with the same number of solo tackles. Courtney had three more tackle for losses, and one more sack than I did, and I had one more interception and three more pass break-ups than Courtney. Combined, our numbers would have been worthy of All-Conference consideration. Separately, we were middle-of-the-pack players. Regardless, I admired Courtney for his selflessness, his work ethic, his friendship, his preparation, and his approach. He was the model teammate, and personification of the skill of seizing the opportunity.

In many instances in life, we never know when occasions may surface that offer an opportunity to bring about change. When they do, we must be ready to capitalize, for the window to act may be narrow, and additional opportunities may be few. Athletics, and teammates like Courtney Rose, provided the backdrop for me to learn such an invaluable lesson.

Courtney Rose was the most unselfish teammate I played with at Auburn. We played the same position, shared adjacent lockers, sat in every meeting together, practiced every technique, trained every repetition, and studied every schematic adjustment beside each other. We had different body types, different skill sets, came from different backgrounds, studied different sciences as majors, yet always respected one another and were always friends. When given the opportunity, Courtney rose to the occasion to propel Auburn to success. His night in Oxford, Mississippi, to begin SEC play in 2000 arose out of my lack of stamina, and Courtney did not disappoint. He starred.

Seize the Moment

By Courtney Rose

When I think back to my time at the Loveliest Village on the Plains, and how I "seized the moment" specifically as an athlete, two specific moments come to mind. The first breakthrough occurred in 1998, in an SEC contest versus the Florida Gators. We played them in the Swamp, in a game that was competitive for about two-and-a-half quarters. I was a red-shirt sophomore who had played mostly special teams up to this point. Because of the personnel and tendencies of Florida's offense, an opportunity to seize the moment had finally arrived.

Our defensive coordinator and defensive back coach at the time was Bill Oliver, a renowned defensive coordinator with one of the best defensive minds in college football, and the accolades to show for it. Trying to match wits with Steve Spurrier, he implemented a dime package that week, which required six DBs. He also implemented a variation off the dime package that included seven DBs. In this variation, I lined up as the middle linebacker, and the intent was to matchup personnel, since Florida ran a lot five-wide receiver sets. I didn't start the game, but I played a significant amount of time. We lost 24–3, but I recorded thirteen tackles in a losing effort.

I'm not a selfish teammate who's all caught up in personal stats; I would have preferred to win the game, but it was a pivotal moment for me, from the standpoint of building my confidence and confirming I could compete in this league. In addition, I wanted to show the coaches that I could compete and be trusted to make plays. The next day, I was called in to Coach Oliver's office, and after two-and-a-half of years of wondering if I could compete in the SEC, he finally gave me the confirmation I was looking for. It went something like, "You did good, three-zero, keep getting better." After finally winning coach's confidence, there were coaching changes at the end of the season, and the process started all over for me!

"Seizing the moment" part two came in 2000, during my senior season. We were in an SEC West battle against Ole Miss, and again we were on the road. Coach Oliver departed after the 1998 season and was replaced by John Lovett, a member of Tommy Tuberville's coaching staff. Tommy Tuberville became the head coach in 1999, and brought his entire coaching staff with him. This was his first game back in Ole Miss since he'd accepted the Auburn head coaching job. There were plenty of storylines and anticipation for this game, given the displeasure from Ole Miss fans in the way Tubbs left Hoddy Toddy land. We were the underdogs that day, unranked versus the No. 19 Rebels. Again, I found myself waiting for an opportunity to prove to Coach Lovett this time that I could play and compete.

My opportunity came at the expense of Rob Pate, who had to deal with dehydration issues and serious cramps. He started the game, but due to the high humidity on that warm, balmy night, Rob was unable to go past the first quarter. I played most of the game that night, and wound up with seven tackles, one interception, and a sack. This time, the good guys were victorious. My confirmation came in a different form this go-around. Instead of coach calling me into his office, I was informed by a trainer the next day that I was voted Defensive SEC Player of the Week. As far as individual accomplishments go, it was the highlight of my career.

Each opportunity for me came about unexpectedly, but I was able to take advantage of my opportunities by not focusing on the lack of playing time, but instead understanding that, in football as in life, your number could be called at any time. I was also more concerned with the team being great, rather than myself. So I understood that if I was prepared when the time came, the team would benefit from it, and maybe, just maybe, I'd pick up an award or an "atta boy" along the way.

CONCLUSION

The Wayward Athlete

Everything I have written in the preceding pages I believe deeply, I have been trained to perfect, and make up the framework of who I am. Athletics undoubtedly has provided the tools to be a success in life by drawing upon the lessons it teaches. What I have also realized in writing this book is that the building blocks athletics has formed in my life have an ironic downfall attached. They gave me the false belief that I can accomplish anything in my own power. If I try harder, dig deeper, work longer, strive painstakingly then I can attain the desired outcome. In and of themselves, these are not bad qualities—these are very good traits. These are the traits that produce successes and the reason this book was written. These are the behaviors that shape young minds into quality adults.

But digging deeper has revealed to me these characteristics are a house of cards built on an unsolid foundation when detached from a healthy heart. I am not good enough in my own power. I cannot tackle this world, the temptations that constantly knock at the door, the battle for doing what is right versus what feels right, the questions that permeate my mind and harden my soul. Sure, a life of athletics has given the tools to be successful in the here and now, but it has failed to give the vulnerability to be successful in the eternal.

I have learned athletics taught me to not show weakness, to hide pain, to be a leader and display strength even when I felt overwhelmed. I have learned my upbringing to be a success in all avenues and my desire and determination to do just that has given me a sense of pride and egocentricity that has prevented me from true joy in my life. The fallacy of closing off, withholding hurts, suppressing pains, pushing beyond discomforts has fashioned an individual unwilling and scared to let others see my mistakes, my flaws, my shames, my imperfection. It has made me into a man that has a difficult time being honest with his fears and anxieties with even those I most love—even me! And it has been a revelation to see it unearthed.

I am not now advocating against all I have written—quite the opposite. I believe wholeheartedly in the principles I have gained through sport. They have served me well in many of life's valleys and quite honestly they have prevented me from finding myself in many of life's valleys. I am grateful for lessons taught on the field and applied in life. But there is a missing ingredient and it is humility. Not the humility I have discussed—that of being a good sport, that of spreading the compliments to teammates, that of placing the team before yourself. Rather I am speaking of a humility of the heart that says, "You are not as powerful, and omniscient, and capable as you think! You are in need of communion, vulnerability, and brokenness—concepts your training has overlooked!"

Obtaining, accepting, acknowledging, and welcoming brokenness is the most freeing and lasting and impactful component of producing a joyful person. Not just an athlete—anyone! During the writing of this book I have been broken for the first time in my life. My eyes have been opened to the inadequacies in which I was blindly living and my pride has been shattered. The athlete in me wants to, has been trained to, fights hard to pick those pieces up in my own strength and rebuild my scaffolding. That's the ego improper humility at the heart level had produced. I now walk in freedom; a freedom that could only come from being broken. I walk in comfort of communion with my Savior knowing he walks before me. I walk into life's challenges knowing I don't walk alone, I can be vulnerable, I can show pain, I can ask for help. That is missing in our athletic upbringing and sending a kid to church camp or hoping the lesson is imparted accidentally will never suffice. The lesson must be intentional and athletes must know it is okay to not be perfect. It is okay to be weak. It is okay to depend on others at the heart level. In short—I am now strong enough to admit I am weak. It took brokenness to find it in my life and I pray I remain broken and surrender my ways to His every single day!

Ezekiel 36:26: "And I will give you a new heart, and I will put a new spirit in you. I will take out the stony heart and give you a tender, responsive heart."